An Assessment of the Investment Climate in South Africa

An Assessment of the Investment Climate in South Africa

George R. G. Clarke
James Habyarimana
Michael Ingram
David Kaplan
Vijaya Ramachandran

THE WORLD BANK
Washington, DC

1818 H Street NW
Washington DC 20433
Telephone: 202-473-1000
Internet: www.worldbank.org
E-mail: feedback@worldbank.org

1 2 3 4 10 09 08 07

ISBN-10: 0-8213-6898-2
ISBN-13: 978-0-8213-6898-5
eISBN: 0-8213-6899-0
eISBN-13: 978-0-8213-6899-2
DOI: 10.1596/978-0-8213-6898-5

Cover photo: Jon Berndt.

Library of Congress Cataloging-in-Publication Data

An assessment of the investment climate in South Africa/George Clarke . . . [et al.].
p. cm.
Includes bibliographical references.
ISBN 978-0-8213-6898-5
ISBN 978-0-8213-6899-2
1. Investments—South Africa. 2. South Africa—Economic conditions—1991—I. Clarke, George R. G.

HG5851.A3A87 2007
330.968—dc22 2006033917

Contents

Figures

Tables

Acknowledgments

We wish to acknowledge the support of the Department of Trade and Industry (DTI), Republic of South Africa. Generous funding by DTI enabled over 800 firms to be interviewed in four major metropolitan areas of South Africa; these interviews provided the basis for the analysis. In particular, we wish to thank Ravi Naidoo and Susan Mashamaite, as well as Norman Munzhelele. Alan Hirsch provided valuable comments. We owe all of the participating firms an enormous debt for their willingness to spend time and share information with us.

The South Africa Investment Climate Survey was entirely enumerated by Citizen Surveys, a survey and market research firm based in Cape Town. We would like to acknowledge the work of Washeelah Kapery, Matthew Schartz, and Reza Omar. John Paton helped prepare the survey, and Jean Michel Marchat carried out the sampling.

We are grateful to Zeljko Bogetic, Alan Gelb, and Jose Reis for comments on earlier versions of the report and would like to acknowledge the extraordinary support and input provided by the World Bank's country director for South Africa, Ritva Reinikka. Benn Eifert contributed significantly to the analysis of the survey data for the first draft of the report. Several other individuals made valuable contributions at different stages of this work: Demba Ba, Vandana Chandra, Pryd Chitah,

Veronica Coetzee, David Dollar, Stephen Gelb, Mary Hallward-Driemeier, Phil Keefer, Augustine Mkandawire, John Nasir, Axel Peuker, Jim Sackey, Ben Smit, Dileep Wagle, Michaela Weber, Giovanni Tanzillo, and Eric Wood.

Executive Summary

The objective of the South Africa Investment Climate Assessment (ICA) is to evaluate the investment climate in South Africa in all its operational dimensions and to promote policies to strengthen the private sector. The investment climate is made up of the many location-specific factors that shape opportunities and incentives for firms to invest productively, create jobs, and expand. These factors include macroeconomic and regulatory policies, the security of property rights and the rule of law, and the quality of supporting institutions such as physical and financial infrastructure.

The main source of information for the ICA is a survey of over 800 formal private enterprises. The survey includes data on firm productivity, the cost of doing business, the regulatory environment, the labor market, the financial sector, the trade regime, and levels of investment. The analysis links business environment constraints to firm-level costs and productivity.

The investment climate and performance of firms in South Africa can be compared with those of firms in the more than 70 low- and middle-income countries in which Investment Climate Surveys (ICSs) have been conducted. For the purpose of this study, the investment climate and firm performance in South Africa are benchmarked against those of two relatively productive countries in Sub-Saharan Africa (Senegal and Kenya); four middle-income countries outside that region (Brazil, Lithuania, Malaysia, and Poland); and China, one of the fastest-growing economies in the world.

In addition to firm-level data from the survey, the ICA draws on additional sources of information, including other data sources from within the World Bank, such as the Doing Business Indicators, and research by the World Bank and other international organizations, the government of South Africa, and academia.

The Survey

Citizen Surveys, a private South African firm based in Cape Town, conducted the ICS. It surveyed about 800 firms between January and December 2004. About 75 percent (603) of these firms are in the manufacturing sector, 14 percent in the construction industry, and the remaining 11 percent in wholesale and retail trade. Within these broad sectors, firms were randomly selected from lists of firms registered with the South Africa Department of Trade and Industry (that is, only formal registered enterprises are included in the sample). Although the firms should be broadly representative of formal firms within each sector, they are not representative of the entire economy. For this reason, and because the samples for comparator countries cover only manufacturing, data from the three sectors are presented separately in the main report.

The sample included firms from major metropolitan areas in Gauteng (about 63 percent of the sample), Western Cape (23 percent), KwaZulu-Natal (9 percent), and Eastern Cape (5 percent). The sample was mainly composed of small (10–49 employees), medium-size (50–99 employees), and large (100–499 employees) enterprises; about 14 percent of the firms were very large (over 500 employees). The sample included only a few micro enterprises (fewer than 10 employees), especially in the manufacturing sector.

Most firms are owned either by corporations (that is, other firms) or white individuals and families. Only 5 percent of firms are owned by black individuals or families or colored[1] individuals or families.The small number of black-owned firms appears to reflect the distribution of formal firms. Previous studies also found relatively few white-owned firms in these size classes. For example, in a survey of enterprises in Johannesburg in 1999, 97 percent of informal micro enterprises but only

7 percent of formal micro, small, and medium-scale enterprises were black-owned (Chandra and others 2001a, 2002b).

Macroeconomic Background

Since the transition to democracy, South Africa's macroeconomic performance has been solid but not spectacular. Between 1994 and 2003, annual gross domestic product (GDP) growth averaged about 2.9 percent, while annual per capita GDP growth averaged less than 1 percent. Although GDP growth fluctuated over this period, it has neither declined nor exceeded 4.5 percent in any calendar year since 1993. In this respect, South Africa appears locked into a path of sustained but moderate growth, particularly in light of growth in comparator countries outside Africa. Between 1994 and 2003, per capita growth was more than 3 times faster in Thailand and Malaysia than in South Africa—despite the Asian financial crisis in the mid-1990s, when GDP dropped by close to 10 percent in these countries—and 10 times faster in China. Given the challenges that South Africa will face and its currently high level of unemployment, faster growth is vital.

Investment has also been low, remaining between about 15 and 16 percent of GDP.[2] This rate is lower than the government's "unofficial" target of 25 percent, lower than in the middle-income comparator countries (Brazil and Poland), and far lower than in the fastest-growing Asian economies. Public sector investment has been low, but private investment, at about 12 percent of GDP, has also been low.

Firm Performance

Despite South Africa's only modestly successful macroeconomic performance, labor productivity is high. In 2002, value added was US$14,000 per worker for the median formal firm in the ICS. This rate is far higher than that in the most productive countries elsewhere in Sub-Saharan Africa and compares well with the rate in other middle-income countries such as Brazil, Lithuania, Malaysia, and Poland—all of which except Brazil have higher per capita income than South Africa. Productivity is also higher than in China—although slightly lower than in the most productive areas of that country.

One reason that South Africa's productivity appears high is that South African enterprises are concentrated in relatively capital-intensive industries. Over the 1980s and 1990s, South African manufacturing became increasingly capital intensive, because firms adopted capital-intensive production methods and expanded into capital-intensive sectors. To partially control for this reality, the present analysis examines labor productivity in a single industry—the garment industry. South African firms appear relatively productive in this sector as well, although the differences are less noticeable than they are for manufacturing overall. Labor productivity in this sector remains higher in South Africa than in other Sub-Saharan African countries, Brazil, China, and Lithuania but slightly lower than in Malaysia or Poland.

Other evidence suggests that enterprises in South Africa are relatively capital intensive. Firms in South Africa have about twice as much capital per worker (about $3,500) as firms in Brazil, the most productive areas of China, and Lithuania. Malaysian and Polish firms had slightly more capital per worker, although the weak rand in 2002 might lead to underestimation of the amount of capital per worker in South Africa.

Per worker labor costs in South Africa, about $7,300 in 2002, are high compared with those in other countries. These costs were equal to about $2,000 in the most productive areas of China, about $2,700 in Brazil and Lithuania, and about $4,000 in Malaysia and Poland. High labor costs mean that South Africa's unit labor costs (labor costs as a percent of value added) are higher than such costs in most of the comparator countries, except those in Eastern Europe.

Despite highly capital-intensive production and high labor costs, labor productivity is high enough to ensure that existing firms are relatively profitable. Profitability (profits over sales) in South African firms was higher than that in firms in Lithuania, Malaysia, or Poland but lower than that in Brazilian firms. At the firm level, profitability is associated with better performance; firms that are more productive and have lower costs will be more profitable than other firms. But at an economy level, high profitability can also suggest a lack of competition; when markets are competitive and entry is possible, profits typically will be competed away.

The Investment Climate

The ICS asked firms to report how serious an obstacle various areas of the investment climate are to enterprise operations and growth. Such perception-based measures suffer from several problems. Comparing them across countries and quantifying and aggregating them across firms are difficult. Moreover, managers might be unaware of the underlying causes of a specific constraint and might have different views from potential entrepreneurs. Nevertheless, enterprise managers probably have a reasonable grasp of the immediate problems facing their businesses. Thus, perception-based indexes provide a useful starting point for the analysis—one supplemented with objective measures of the investment climate presented throughout this volume.

One interesting feature of the South African data is that relatively few firms rated the constraints as major or very severe. Only about 35 percent of firms rated the biggest constraint, worker skills, as a serious problem, and fewer than one in five enterprises—far fewer than in most countries—rated most obstacles a serious concern. By comparison, 85 percent of firms in Brazil said that tax rates were a major problem and 74 percent of firms in Kenya said that corruption was a major problem. The findings suggest that enterprise managers in South Africa are not overly concerned about any area of the investment climate.

However, four areas of the investment climate—worker skills, macroeconomic instability, labor regulations, and crime—stand out as particular problems. Between 29 and 35 percent of enterprises rated each of these areas major problems, whereas less than 20 percent rated other areas major problems.

A few differences between types of firms are noticeable when firms are broken down by ownership, export status, foreign participation, province, or sector. The most noticeable differences are that exporters were far more concerned about macroeconomic stability than other firms and that black-owned firms were far more concerned about access to and the cost of financing than other firms.

Worker Skills

Enterprise managers were more likely to say that worker skills were a serious obstacle to operations and growth than any other area of the investment climate. Consistent with the perception-based indexes, additional questions on the ICS elicited evidence that firms have difficulty attracting skilled workers.

First, they appear to pay a high premium for skilled and educated workers. Econometric analysis of individual workers' wages suggests that returns from schooling are high. Before controlling for occupational status (for example, whether the worker is unskilled, skilled, or a manager), an additional year of education is associated with a 12 percent increase in wages. Even after controlling for occupational status (for example, assuming that education does not affect whether the worker is skilled or unskilled), an additional year of education is associated with a 6.5 to 7.0 percent increase in wages.

Second, wages appear to be relatively higher for managers and skilled workers than for unskilled workers in South Africa. The median monthly wage for an unskilled production worker in South Africa in 2002 was about $240 per month. By comparison, an unskilled worker in Poland earns about $250 per month, and an unskilled worker in Brazil earns about $167 per month. The median monthly wage for a manager in South Africa is about $1,850 per month—over twice as high as in Poland ($740 per month) and over three times as high as in Brazil ($540 per month). South African managers earn nine times as much as unskilled workers compared with three times as much for Brazilian and Polish managers and about two times as much for Chinese managers. High wages in South Africa appear to be mainly due to high wages for managers and professionals and not to high wages at the bottom of the income distribution.

Despite concerns about worker skills, relatively few enterprises had training programs. According to firm managers, between 60 and 80 percent of unskilled and skilled workers in Brazil, China, and Poland receive training. By contrast, fewer than half of workers in South Africa receive training. The actual percentage could be lower. When asked about formal training, more than 80 percent of workers in South Africa reported that they had received none. Foreign-owned firms, exporters, and large firms are more likely than other firms to provide training.

Workers who had been trained reported that their wages were 15 to 20 percent higher than untrained workers. To the extent that higher wages reflect that trained workers are more productive, the return to training—at least for workers—could be high.

But trained workers might receive higher wages for other reasons. Managers might select the most productive workers to receive training—either because they think these workers will benefit more from training or because they use training to reward their best workers. Other evidence is consistent with this second explanation; firms that have training programs appear to be no more productive than firms without such programs.

Given the large number of firms that provide no training, government agencies and programs responsible for encouraging training will be crucial in raising human capital levels in South Africa. To date, these agencies and programs have been unsuccessful. Fewer firms have training programs in South Africa than firms in other middle-income countries, and evidence that training increases worker productivity is mixed.

Labor Regulation

Although the ICS asked detailed questions related to labor costs and worker skills, it included few objective indicators of labor regulation. Therefore, the information in the survey is supplemented with information from the World Bank's Doing Business database. The database includes several indexes that measure the rigidity of hiring and firing regulations and the cost of firing (World Bank 2004d).[3] Consistent with the perception-based indexes, labor regulation in South Africa is more rigid than in most of the comparator countries on both the hiring and firing indexes. That is, hiring and firing workers is more costly and difficult in South Africa than in most of the comparator countries or than in most Organization for Economic Cooperation and Development (OECD) economies. However, on one particular measure, the cost of firing an individual in weeks of wages, South Africa performs relatively well. The cost in South Africa is 38 weeks, lower than the average for the OECD and several of the comparator countries.

Macroeconomic Instability

Thirty-three percent of firms rated macroeconomic instability as a serious obstacle to enterprise operations and growth—making it the second greatest constraint identified through the ICS. Although growth has been positive for over a decade and inflation modest, exchange rates have been unstable. Between 2000 and 2002, the rand depreciated against most major currencies, falling by about 26 percent against the British pound, 27 percent against the U.S. dollar, and 28 percent against the euro in real terms. But between 2002 and 2004 it appreciated 29 percent against the euro, 35 percent against the pound, and 67 percent against the dollar in real terms.

The idea that rapid fluctuations in the exchange rate engender the perception that macroeconomic instability is a serious problem is consistent with the finding that exporters were far more concerned about the macroeconomy than nonexporters. Forty-four percent of exporters rated macroeconomic instability a major or very severe problem, compared with only 28 percent of nonexporters. Because many South African manufacturing firms appear to be price takers in international markets, changes in the exchange rate can have a serious impact on enterprise revenues. Moreover, nearly three-quarters of exporters to the United States—the country with the currency against which the rand has been most unstable—viewed macroeconomic instability as a major concern. These results strongly suggest that exchange rate instability is firms' main concern with respect to the macroeconomy.

Crime

In South Africa, rates of violent crime, especially murder, have declined modestly, but other crimes—particularly property crimes—have been increasing (Leggett 2003). Between 1994 and 2000, common robbery increased by 168 percent and aggravated robbery increased by 31 percent (Altbeker 2001). About 44 percent of blacks and 58 percent of whites cited crime as the most serious problem facing South Africa in the mid-1990s (NEDCOR 1996).

Evidence from the ICS suggests that crime is also a serious concern for business. The median firm reported that the direct losses due to crime and the cost of security were equal to about 0.5 percent of sales, which is higher than in many middle-income countries, including China, Lithuania, and Poland, but lower than in Brazil and Kenya, where median costs were equal to about 1 percent of sales, and in Ecuador, where these costs were equal to about 5 percent of sales.

Security costs account for about 60 percent and direct losses for about 40 percent of the cost of crime. Protection payments to organized crime were very low in South Africa, compared with many middle-income countries in Asia and Eastern Europe.

The burden of crime is not evenly distributed across firms. In general, firms involved in retail and wholesale trade faced the biggest losses; firms in the manufacturing sector faced the lowest losses. Large firms tended to sustain higher losses than smaller firms. After controlling for other factors, firms in KwaZulu-Natal faced the heaviest losses; firms in Gauteng sustained relatively modest losses.

Finance

Enterprise managers often view access to and the cost of financing as serious obstacles to operations and growth. In Sub-Saharan Africa, access to and cost of financing typically rank among the top five constraints. Yet firms in South Africa were generally far less concerned about financing; fewer than 20 percent rated either access or cost as a major or very severe obstacle, making them 8th and 11th of 18 constraints.

Objective data generally support the perception-based data—particularly with respect to the cost of financing. The real interest rates that firms reported paying for their most recent loan were lower than the rates in most of the comparator countries for which data were available.

Although the formal firms in the survey were relatively unconcerned about access to financing, they did not appear awash with bank credit. Firms in South Africa finance less investment through banks than firms in most of the comparator countries (for example, China, Kenya, Poland, and Senegal), and fewer firms in South Africa have overdraft facilities than firms in either Brazil or Kenya. Moreover, South African firms rely heavily on retained earnings to finance both investment and working capital.

Why do South African firms rely so little on external sources to finance investment? The main reason appears to be that firms have little demand for external credit, rather than that supply is limited. Most firms without loans reported that they did not want or need a loan, and very few firms had been rejected for a loan.

As noted above, black-owned firms were far more concerned about access to and the cost of financing than white-owned firms—even after controlling for other observable differences that might affect perceptions about financing, such as enterprise size, sector of operation, and age.

The objective measures of financing provide some support for the idea that obtaining access to credit is more difficult for black-owned firms. These firms were less likely to have ever applied for or to have received a loan and to have an overdraft facility. They were more likely to have been rejected for a loan and to have paid higher interest rates on their loans.

Although these measures might suggest discrimination, some provisos must be kept in mind. First, the differences could be due to random sample variation and are often modest. Second, they could be due to unobservable differences among firms, such as the availability of collateral or the business experience of the firms' management teams.

AIDS

In addition to being catastrophic in terms of lost lives and health, HIV/AIDS also undermines economic development. The International Monetary Fund identifies HIV/AIDS as one of the two main potential constraints on future growth in South Africa.

Firms were asked to evaluate the impact of the HIV epidemic on various measures of firm performance. In general, firms were only moderately concerned about the immediate impact of the epidemic. Only about 6 percent of firms reported that the epidemic was having a strong impact on labor productivity, and only 4 percent reported a strong impact on profits. The greatest immediate impact appeared to be on employee absenteeism; nearly one-quarter of firms estimated that the epidemic increased absenteeism by more than 5 percent.

Firms do appear to be concerned about the medium-term impact of the epidemic; about 45 percent reported that the epidemic had a strong impact on firm investment. This perception is potentially driven by increased uncertainty about the impact that the epidemic will have on productivity, market size, and profitability.

The survey results also suggest that workers are aware of the problem. Nearly two-thirds of workers reported that they were concerned about it, and nearly 95 percent reported that they knew where they could get tested. But only half reported that they were willing to be tested, which probably reflects concern about stigma and about the availability or cost of comprehensive treatment programs.

Competition

Previous research has suggested that the South African economy is highly concentrated and that barriers to entry are high for both domestic and foreign firms. Consistent with this finding, firms in South Africa appear to be relatively profitable despite high wages. High observed wages could also be consistent with the observation that the market is highly concentrated if managers, owners, and workers share the rents created by low levels of competition. Directly assessing the importance of competition using firm-level data is difficult, because firms rarely complain about a lack of competition, and asking objective questions to assess the state of competition is difficult.

Other Areas of the Investment Climate

Firms had few complaints about most other areas of the investment climate. Few firms rated infrastructure, regulation, taxation, corruption, or the court system as serious obstacles. The objective indicators are generally consistent with the perception-based measures. Most firms believe that courts can enforce property rights, and court cases appear to be resolved relatively quickly. Losses due to power outages are modest, and the cost of power is low by international standards. Tax rates are low and have been decreasing. Although the burden of regulation is not particularly low, it is lower than in most countries in Africa and is comparable to that in most middle-income countries. Few firms report paying bribes to obtain services or win government contracts. In summary, South Africa appears to perform relatively well in most other areas of the investment climate.

Summary

Why was investment and growth in South Africa low between 1994 and 2003? Firm productivity is relatively high, and objective indicators show that the investment climate is mostly favorable—power is cheap and relatively reliable, the burden of regulation is not excessive, corruption is low, ports function relatively well, access to finance does not appear to be a major problem for most enterprises, and most people trust the court system. The puzzle simply stated is the following: If firms are relatively productive and the investment climate is favorable, why has private investment been so modest?

The analysis presented in this volume suggests several possible answers. First, some areas of the investment climate are not favorable. The exchange rate has been unstable (chapter 1), which is especially problematic for exporters; the cost of labor is high, especially for skilled workers (chapter 3); labor regulation is burdensome (chapter 3); and the cost of crime is high (chapter 5). All these factors discourage investment.

Second, the investment climate has improved in recent years. Interest rates and inflation have fallen (chapter 1), corporate tax rates have decreased (chapter 5), and profits generally have increased (chapter 2). Investment rates, although lower than would have been expected given the broadly favorable investment climate, have begun to increase.

Finally, other areas of the investment climate not well captured in the firm survey might deter investment. In particular, market concentration and systemic risk—two factors that are difficult to pick up in firm-level surveys—are likely to affect firm performance and investment.

Notes

1. The term *colored* is largely used in South Africa for people of mixed race. These people include slaves brought in from East and Central Africa; the indigenous Khoisan who lived at the Cape during the age of slavery; indigenous African blacks; whites (mainly Dutch/Afrikaner and British settlers); and people of mixed Javanese, Malay, Indian, Malagasy, European (such as Portuguese), and Asian (such as Burmese) blood.
2. Data are from the South African Reserve Bank download facility Time Series KBP6282J.
3. South Africa was misclassified in early versions of the Doing Business database due to calculation errors and a change in methodology. These errors have been corrected in the most recent Doing Business reports.

Abbreviations

BCEA	Basic Conditions of Employment Act
BEE	Black economic empowerment (transactions) and Black Economic Empowerment Act
CIT	Company Income Tax
EEA	Equity Employment Act
ICAs	investment climate assessments
ICSs	Investment Climate Surveys
ICT	information and communication technology
LFS	Labor Force Survey
LRA	Labor Relations Act
OECD	Organisation for Economic Co-operation and Development
SACU	Southern African Customs Union
SDA	Skills Development Act
SETAs	training agencies set up by the South African government
SME	small and medium-size enterprise
STC	Secondary Tax on Companies
TFP	total factor productivity

CHAPTER 1

Macroeconomic Background

Investment climate plays a major role in promoting market-led growth and reducing poverty (Stern 2002a, 2002b). Improving living standards and reducing poverty depend on broad-based economic growth, which will occur only when firms improve worker productivity by investing in human and physical capital and technological capacity (defined broadly to include investment in knowledge, equipment, and organizational structure). But firms will only invest when the investment climate is favorable.

The investment climate includes economic incentives, which are shaped by macroeconomic and regulatory policies and public administrative procedures and by institutional incentives, such as the security of property rights, the rule of law, and governance stability.[1] Institutional arrangements influence private investment decisions by structuring the rules of the game. These rules affect investment uncertainty and risk as well as investment safeguards (protection of property rights, enforcement of contracts, and maintenance of integrity of monetary standards). Defined in this manner, the investment climate determines the returns from different economic activities.

Much of the analysis presented in this report is based on an Investment Climate Survey (ICS) of 800 South African firms in 2004. The data generated by this survey, developed by the World Bank in 2001, allow analysis of several factors: firm performance as measured by firm-level productivity; characteristics of factor markets, such as labor and finance; and the impact of the business environment, including infrastructure, regulation, crime, and security. Because the ICS is administered in a standardized manner and targeted at roughly comparable subsectors in manufacturing, it shows how South African firms perform relative to their counterparts around the world, and what their constraints are in a comparative context.[2]

Over the last decade, South Africa has experienced sustained, albeit moderate, growth. Investment has been low, in part because public sector investment has been low and in part because private sector investment has also been limited. Consequently, fixed capital augmentation has contributed only modestly to growth. President Thabo Mbeki has recently established a high-level task team to achieve a step-wise increase in South Africa's growth rate. The president has identified raising the rate of investment as the key to achieving higher growth.

The president's initiative has received widespread support, but views on what factors restrain investment, and therefore how higher rates of investment might best be accomplished, vary. Competing explanations include the exchange rate, skill shortages, public infrastructure, high rates of taxation, business regulation, and health policy.

ICS results show that South African firms face a mostly favorable investment climate. Power is cheap and relatively reliable, the burden of regulation is not excessive, corruption is low, ports function relatively well, access to finance does not appear to be a major problem for most enterprises, and most people trust the court system. But if the investment climate is so favorable, why has the private sector's investment response not been stronger?

Although most factors are favorable, some problems remain. The exchange rate has been unstable, imposing high costs on exporters; the cost of labor is high, especially for skilled workers (chapter 3); labor regulation is burdensome (chapter 3); and the cost of crime is high (chapter 5). All these factors discourage investment, despite the generally favorable climate in other areas.

In addition, some improvements in the investment climate have been recent. Interest rates and inflation have fallen (chapter 1), and corporate tax rates have been reduced (chapter 5). Moreover, these improvements have occurred within the context of generally increasing profits (chapter 2). Thus, investment rates, although lower than would have been expected given the broadly favorable investment climate, have begun to rise.

Finally, other areas of the investment climate not captured well by the ICS might deter investment. In particular, both market concentration and systematic risk—two factors that are difficult to pick up in firm-level surveys—are likely to affect firm performance and investment.

This chapter examines the macroeconomic environment in South Africa at the time of survey. It presents a brief examination of South Africa's economic growth, examines corporate investment rates, and reviews the financing of investment, notably through savings. It discusses two variables with a strong impact on corporate investment: interest rates and exchange rates. The chapter then returns to the issue of the lower-than-expected but improving rate of investment.

Economic Growth

In the last decade of apartheid, the economy grew at 1.1 percent per year. The growth rate averaged 2.9 percent per year from 1994 to 2003 and 2.7 percent per year between 1998 and 2003.[3] In 2004 growth was 3.7 percent (*Financial Mail* 2005, 36). Although the growth rate has fluctuated, no decrease has occurred in any calendar year since 1993. On the other hand, growth has not exceeded 4.5 percent in any year. South Africa appears locked into a path of sustained but moderate growth.

Because South Africa's population has been increasing, per capita growth has been slower than total growth. Per capita growth has been modest relative to that in comparator countries outside Africa, especially the fast-growing Asian economies (see figure 1.1). Over the past decade,

Figure 1.1 Cross-Country Comparison of per Capita Growth, 1994–2003

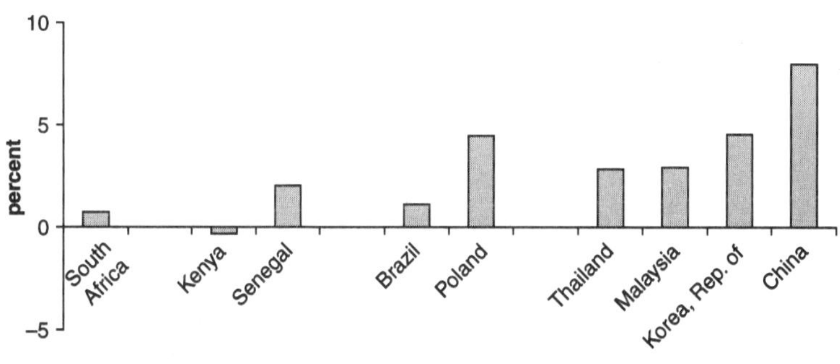

Source: World Bank 2005b.

Table 1.1 Reuters Consensus Forecast for Real GDP Growth for South Africa, 2005–07

	2005	*2006*	*2007*
Real GDP growth	4.0	3.6	4.0
Highest forecast	4.5	4.3	4.9
Lowest forecast	3.5	3.2	3.1

Source: Reuters Consensus Forecast.

per capita growth has been over 3 times faster in Thailand and Malaysia than in South Africa—despite the Asian crisis in the mid-1990s—and has been nearly 10 times faster in China.[4]

However, South Africa may be breaking out of its moderate growth cycle. At the time of the survey, many economists were forecasting higher growth rates (table 1.1).[5] Actual growth, reaching 4.8 percent in 2005 (World Bank 2005b), appears to have exceeded these forecasts.

In the short term, higher growth will be heavily dependent on two major factors: the value of the rand and maintenance of historically higher dollar prices for South African commodity exports. However, infrastructural and skill bottlenecks could occur if the economy were to sustain high growth rates for any extended period.

In terms of sectoral contribution to GDP over the last decade, the outstanding feature has been a shift to the tertiary and services sectors (table 1.2). From 1998 to 2003, the primary sectors—manufacturing, construction, and electricity and water—experienced some decrease. The share of government services also decreased. The transport and communications sector and the finance, real estate, and business services sector increased their shares.

Within manufacturing, the share of labor-intensive sectors (food and beverages, textiles, clothing and footwear) declined significantly.[7] Within the tertiary sector, the government share declined, but the shares of financial and business services and transport and communications significantly increased. In 2004 wholesale and retail trade, hotels and restaurants (6.5 percent), construction (6.3 percent), and transport and communications (5.5 percent) made the most significant contribution to GDP growth.

Investment and Savings

The investment climate shapes firms' incentives to invest and individuals' incentives to save. Investment and savings in South Africa at the time of the survey are examined below in both a cross-country and historical context.

Table 1.2 Sectoral Composition of GDP, 1998–2003

	Agriculture	*Mining*	*Manu-facturing*	*Electricity and water*	*Construction*	*Trade, hotels, restaurants*	*Transport, communi-cations*	*Finance, real estate, business services*	*Community, social, personal services*	*Government services*
1998	4.2	6.5	20.1	3.8	3.2	13.7	10.1	17.9	2.6	15.3
2003	4.0	5.5	19.8	3.5	3.1	13.7	12.2	19.6	2.7	13.1

Sources: Statistics South Africa; *Bulletin of Statistics* 2004.
Note: National accounts GDP by industry are at constant 1995 prices.

Fixed Investment

In the 1970s and 1980s, capital investment and employment creation accounted for most growth. In the 1990s, a decline in employment and low investment meant labor augmentation contributed negatively and capital investment contributed only weakly to growth. The strongest contributor to growth in the 1990s was productivity growth due to technological change (Fedderke 2005, 9).

The International Monetary Fund (IMF), which estimated South Africa's potential GDP growth at 3 percent per year, has similarly argued that increased productivity, rather than growth in labor and capital inputs, is the main contributor to growth. The IMF contends that productivity growth arises from the lowering of trade barriers, increased exposure to international trade, and the private sector's increased share in fixed investment that raises the productivity of capital. It identifies two major constraints on potential growth: the HIV/AIDS epidemic and the availability of skilled labor (IMF 2004).

In the decade before 1994, investment in South Africa declined by 3 percent per year, but in the next decade, it rose by some 5 percent per year. However, the overall magnitude of investment—private sector and government—remained between 15 and 16 percent of GDP.[8] Although comparable to capital formation in Kenya and Senegal (the comparator countries in Sub-Saharan Africa), this magnitude of investment is lower than that in Brazil and Poland (the middle-income comparator countries) and far lower than that in the fast-growing Asian economies (figure 1.2). Gross fixed capital formation increased by 9 percent in 2003 and

Figure 1.2 Cross-Country Comparison of Gross Fixed Capital Formation, Average 1994–2003

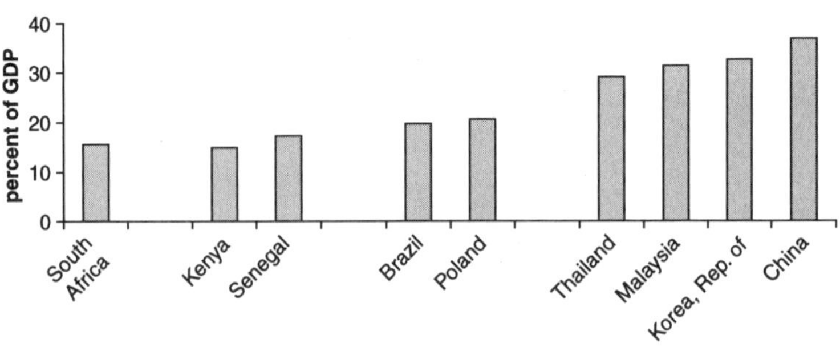

Source: World Bank 2005b.

7.5 percent in 2004 but remained lower than that in the fast-growing Asian economies.

By contrast with the historical analysis of the longer-term determinants of economic growth in South Africa, the National Treasury's analysis suggests that increased fixed investment has principally driven recent economic growth (National Treasury 2005, 11). The Treasury indicates that capital formation will be the principal driver of enhanced growth and forecasts it to rise far more rapidly than the other components of GDP (table 1.3).

On the private sector's part, fixed investment rose from a very low base between 1994 and 1997. After the emerging market crisis in 1998 and 1999, capital formation by private business enterprises declined significantly. Since that time, however, investment by private enterprises has steadily increased (table 1.4). The rise in private sector fixed investment accelerated significantly during 2004, increasing at an annual rate of 13 percent in the third quarter. Many sectors have announced big capital expenditure plans, including mining (notably platinum), automotive and chemicals in manufacturing, retail, real estate, and tourism. This rising trend appears set to continue.

Through much of the past decade, public fixed investment has been very limited, and net investment on the part of public corporations has often

Table 1.3 Macroeconomic Outlook Summary, 2004–07 (percentage change)

	2004 Actual	*2005*	*2006*	*2007*
Household consumption	5.9	4.7	3.7	4.2
Capital formation	7.5	7.0	6.2	7.8
Exports	5.0	4.7	3.6	5.7
Imports	12.7	5.9	5.5	5.7
Gross domestic product	3.7	4.3	3.8	4.4

Source: National Treasury 2005, 12 (table 1.1).

Table 1.4 Gross Fixed Capital Formation by Private Enterprises, 1994–2003 (constant 2000 prices)

	1994	*1995*	*1996*	*1997*	*1998*	*1999*	*2000*	*2001*	*2002*	*2003*
Rand (millions)	77,789	86,279	92,974	97,463	95,586	92,559	100,097	106,482	109,118	113,285
% change over previous year	—	11	8	5	−2	−3	8	6	2	4

Source: South African Reserve Bank 2002, 2004b.
Note: Includes transfer costs.

Table 1.5 Private Business Enterprise Share of Capital Formation, 1994–2003

Percent	*1994*	*1995*	*1996*	*1997*	*1998*	*1999*	*2000*	*2002*	*2002*	*2003*
Gross capital formation	78	73	74	71	65	72	74	74	76	71
Net capital formation	134	108	98	88	59	92	102	102	98	73

Source: South African Reserve Bank 2002, 2004b.

been negative. In 2003 the government reversed the secular contraction in capital spending, particularly on the part of public corporations, announcing its intention to support major new investment projects over the next five years in many key infrastructure areas—especially electricity and transport, with an investment of R165 billion planned for Eskom, the state-owned electricity monopoly, and Transnet, the state-owned transportation entity responsible for rail, air, and ports. The net result is that private enterprises have played a dominant role in capital formation, as shown in table 1.5; government began playing a larger role in 2003.

Significant fluctuations in sectoral shares of gross fixed capital formation have occurred. Shares of manufacturing and electricity, gas, and water have declined, while the share of transport and communications has increased (table 1.6).

Despite increases, investment spending remains low. Private investment spending averaged 12.1 percent of GDP between 1994 and 2003 (Gelb 2001). At 16 percent, gross fixed capital formation is lower than the government's "unofficial" target of 25 percent and far lower than that in the fastest-growing economies in Asia. Such formation is also well below the levels required to lift South Africa into a high growth bracket.

Optimists point to several factors that could sustain the current acceleration and allow South Africa to approach the 25 percent target: higher levels of government spending "crowding in" further investment on the part of the private sector, growing confidence in government economic policies, a steady decline in perceptions of political risk, and lower local costs for imported plants and equipment. These positive factors are reflected in rapidly rising business confidence, which is at its highest level since 1980. Private fixed investment spending is generally strongly correlated with business confidence.

Saving

Gross savings as a share of GDP have remained between 15 and 17 percent since 1994, as shown in table 1.7. Corporate sector saving, which declined

Table 1.6 Gross Fixed Capital Formation by Type of Economic Activity, 1994–2003

	1994	*1995*	*1996*	*1997*	*1998*	*1999*	*2000*	*2001*	*2002*	*2003*
Agriculture	4	3.8	4.6	3.8	3.2	3.0	2.9	2.9	3.4	2.9
Mining	9	8.5	8.2	8.7	9.0	9.3	9.9	10.3	11.3	10.4
Manufacturing	23	25	22.9	22.2	20.7	22.3	21.7	22.3	20.8	19.6
Electric, gas, water	7.4	8.1	8.3	7.6	5.5	4.9	3.9	3.7	4.0	4.8
Construction			1	1	1	1.2	1.5	1.4	1.6	1.5
Trade and accommodation			6.5	5.8	5.6	8.4	7.1	7.3	6.6	6.3
Transportation, communications			10	11.5	17.6	14.3	13.3	13.5	13.5	13.6
Finance, real estate, business services			23.9	24.3	22.2	21.6	22.3	22.0	22.1	21.3
Community, social business service			14.7	15.0	15.0	16.2	17.5	16.5	16.7	19.4

Source: South African Reserve Bank 2002, 2004b.

Table 1.7 Corporate Saving and Gross Saving, 1994–2003 (ratio of gross saving to GDP in current prices)

Year	*Corporate saving (R millions)*	*Gross saving (R millions)*	*Corporate saving/gross saving (%)*	*Ratio of gross saving to GDP (%)*
1994	36,750	81,394	45	16.88
1995	35,731	90,568	39	16.52
1996	45,035	99,758	45	16.14
1997	40,367	103,865	39	15.15
1998	32,014	113,127	28	15.24
1999	31,673	129,132	25	15.87
2000	39,918	145,551	27	15.78
2001	27,415	155,678	18	15.26
2002	49,696	198,465	25	16.73
2003	52,166	203,635	26	16.27

Source: South African Reserve Bank download facility Time Series KBP6201J, KBP62031J, and KBP6286J.

significantly after 1996, has picked up strongly since 2002. Gross saving by the corporate sector was 11.5 percent in 2003 (South African Reserve Bank various years).

A lack of savings does not appear to have constrained business investment. Domestic saving was sufficient to finance capital formation in all but two years between 1994 and 2003. Corporate savings were sufficient to fund corporate investment; the corporate sector had an excess of savings over investment between 1994 and 2001 and a near balance through 2004 (Gelb 2004, 388).

This situation may change. If there were to be a significant increase in investment and more especially if this increase were to occur at a time of rising household expenditures combined with rising government expenditures, domestic sources would be limited and financing would rely on significant capital inflows. In 2004 corporate investments increased rapidly. Rising household expenditures and weaker savings levels on the part of government have meant that South Africa has had to rely on foreign resources to finance capital formation. In 2004 foreign inflows were relatively high, at nearly 4 percent of GDP (South African Reserve Bank 2004a, 10).

Interest Rates and Inflation

Real interest rates were clearly on the rise by 1994, but after 1998 they trended downward, apart from a brief spike in 2001. Given that the rate at which firms borrow is generally declining, the concern of firms

Figure 1.3 Nominal and Real Overdraft Rates, 1991–2004

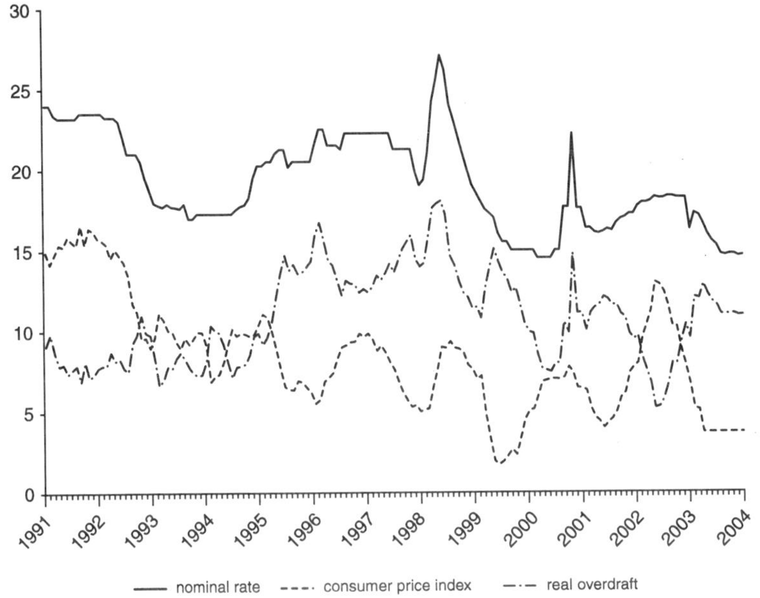

Source: World Bank.

about macroeconomic variables relates principally to the exchange rate (see chapter 5).

Although inflation spiked in 2002–03, before falling in 2004–05, it was between 5 and 10 percent between 1993 and 2003. Thus, although not especially high by international standards, inflation in South Africa remains higher than inflation in the best-performing economies. The recent improvement suggests that inflation might have less of an impact in the short term than it has had over past decades.

Exchange Rate

The exchange rate is rated the second most serious constraint to enterprise operations and growth (chapter 5). Between 2000 and 2002, the trade-weighted real exchange rate depreciated by about 25 percent. The rand depreciated against most major currencies over this period, falling by about 27 percent against the U.S. dollar, 26 percent against the British pound, and 28 percent against the euro in real terms (see figure 1.4).[9] Over the next two years, the rand appreciated against all major currencies, especially the U.S. dollar. Between 2002 and 2004, in the two years prior

Figure 1.4 South Africa's Real Exchange Rate, 1998–2004

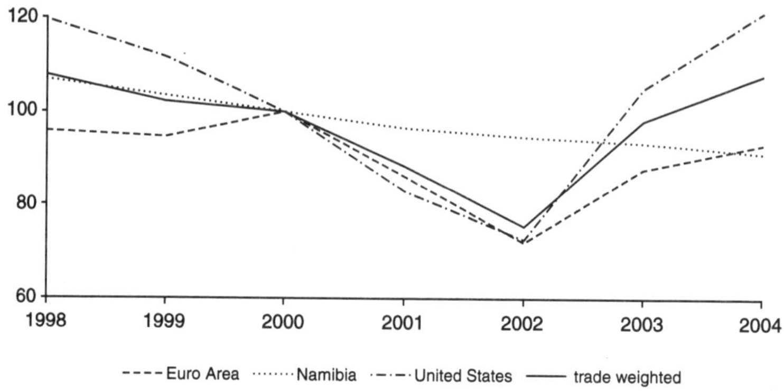

Source: IMF 2005.
Note: Bilateral real exchange rates are calculated relative to 2000 (that is, are equal to 100 in 2000 for all currencies) from the formula from Hinkle and Montiel (1999, 45) using the Consumer Price Index as the measure of inflation. Real exchange rate differences with Namibia are due to differences in inflation in South Africa and Namibia.

to the survey, it appreciated 29 percent against the euro, 35 percent against the British pound, and 67 percent against the U.S. dollar in real terms. Since mid-2001, the Rand has possibly been the most volatile currency openly traded in global markets (Gelb 2004b, 8). Because the precipitous decline and subsequent appreciation of the currency were contrary to nearly all established economists' forecasts, businesses made investment and operational decisions on anticipated exchange rates that were often wide of the mark.

Conclusion

A generally favorable investment climate has not resulted in higher levels of private sector investment in South Africa. One possible explanation relates to new capital formation that occurs as a consequence of new business start-ups. Aggregate fixed investment arises from the investment activities of existing firms as well as new start-up firms. The World Bank's Investment Climate Survey is designed to measure the climate for established firms; new (and potential) entrants may face very different obstacles and constraints. For example, considerable anecdotal evidence suggests that new start-ups have much more difficulty than established firms in accessing finance at reasonable rates, particularly in the absence of substantive collateral due to low income and education levels. The South African system may therefore function relatively well for those that have already secured a place within it but not provide the support needed by new entrants.

A second possible explanation relates to a factor that affects established firms but that is not readily captured in an ICS (for example, the extent to which level of market concentration affects firm-level performance and investment). Some research suggests that the South African economy is highly concentrated and imposes high barriers to entry (to both domestic and foreign firms). Although high levels of concentration reduce firm-level performance, their impact on investment is ambiguous (Fedderke and Szalontai 2005).

A third possible explanation may relate to the nature of investment. Significant shares of investment funds are currently being used to finance Black Economic Empowerment (BEE) transactions. These transactions generally relate to equity transfers rather than investments in the creation of new capital stock. Financial support for BEE transactions is extensive; in 2002 finance made available for BEE was estimated at around R40 billion. Total fixed capital investment in that year was around R175 billion. However, not all BEE finance will be at the "expense" of productive investments. Moreover, financing for BEE only became significant after 2002; low levels of investment have been of longer duration.

A final possible explanation may relate to specification of a key magnitude: risk. Many studies have pointed to systemic risk as the principal factor in declining investment and "waiting" behavior on the part of potential investors (Fedderke 2005). Notoriously diffuse, uncertainty is subject to informational failures and is difficult to measure. The ICS specification of systemic uncertainty may be inadequate.

ICS data can provide no definitive evidence to support any of these potential explanations. However, the survey shows that South Africa's investment climate could be improved in many areas. South Africa has witnessed a significant increase in investment activity by the private sector in response to an improvement in the investment climate. Further improvements should similarly elicit a favorable response in firm performance and investment. But substantially raising the investment rate to support a major increase in the growth rate will require the government to consider some other factors that might have an impact on capital investment.

Notes

1. The term *investment climate*, broadly defined, includes a country's unique attributes or "geography" (climate, endowment of natural resources, distance

from important markets, and so on), as well as the state of its infrastructure, economic and social policies, institutions, and governance stability. This report uses a narrower definition that focuses on the endogenous determinants of investment—for example, "the policy, institutional, and behavioral environment, present and expected, that influences the returns, and risks, associated with investment" (Stern 2002b).

2. In countries where multiple rounds of ICS have been conducted (typically once every three years), researchers can analyze how firms perform over time and how policy changes affect them. Further enumeration in South Africa will enable this analysis to be extended to analysis of the entry and exit of firms in the sample.
3. South Africa released statistics that revised GDP estimates in November 2004. It revised nominal GDP upward some 3.5 percent. Nominal GDP for 2003 is currently estimated at R1251 billion. Recent growth rate estimates were similarly revised upward.
4. The National Treasury estimates average real household income to have increased by 30 percent over the last decade (National Treasury 2005b).
5. The Treasury forecast is for the economy to grow by an average of 4.2 percent over the next few years (National Treasury 2005b). In recent statements, the Minister of Finance has suggested that much higher growth is possible—a figure of 6 percent has been mentioned.
6. The share of these sectors in manufacturing value added decreased from 23 to 20 percent between 1990 and 2000 (Kaplan 2003).
7. Data are from the South African Reserve Bank download facility Time Series KBP6282J.
8. The bilateral real exchange rate against the euro is calculated using consumer price index inflation for Germany.

CHAPTER 2

An Analysis of Firm Performance

The analysis contained in this chapter is based largely on the Investment Climate Survey (ICS) conducted in 2004 by Citizen Surveys. Surveyed firms are located in or near South Africa's major metropolitan areas, including Johannesburg, Cape Town, Port Elizabeth, and Durban. The sample was composed of firms in manufacturing, construction, and retail and wholesale trade. Within these broad sectors, firms were randomly selected from lists of firms registered with the Department of Trade and Industry (only formal registered enterprises are included in the sample). Although broadly representative of formal firms within each sector, the sample is not representative of the entire economy. In the absence of appropriate weights, data cannot be pooled across broad sectors to achieve an economywide representative sample. For this reason, and because the samples for comparator country ICSs cover only manufacturing, data from the three sectors are presented separately.[1]

As shown in table 2.1, about 75 percent (603) of the 803 firms in the sample are in manufacturing. About two-thirds of firms in the sample are based in Gauteng; the remaining firms are based in Western Cape, KwaZulu-Natal, and Eastern Cape. The sample was mainly composed of small (10–49 employees), medium-size (50–99 employees), and large (100–499 employees) enterprises; very large firms (over 500 employees)

Table 2.1 Characteristics of Sample (803 Enterprises) for Investment Climate Survey

	Percent		*Percent*
Geographic distribution:		**Enterprise size:**	
Gauteng	63	Micro (1–9 workers)	5
Western Cape	23	Small (10–49 workers)	27
KwaZulu-Natal	9	Medium-size (50–99 workers)	23
Eastern Cape	5	Large (100–499 workers)	31
		Very large (500 or more workers)	14
Ownership:			
Corporate	40	**Sectors:**	
Individual—European/Caucasian	49	Manufacturing	75
Individual—Asian	6	Construction	14
Individual—African/other	5	Trade (wholesale and retail)	11

Source: Investment Climate Survey.

represent about 14 percent of the sample. Few microenterprises (fewer than 10 employees), especially in the manufacturing sector, are in the sample.

Most firms were owned either by corporations (that is, other firms) or by white individuals and families. Only 5 percent of firms were owned by black or colored individuals or families. The small number of black-owned firms, however, appears to reflect the distribution of formal firms. Previous studies have also found relatively few black-owned firms in these size classes. For example, in a survey of enterprises in Johannesburg in 1999, 97 percent of informal microenterprises but only 7 percent of formal micro, small, and medium-size enterprises were black owned (Chandra and others 2001a, 2002). This pattern appears to have persisted through 2004.

Productivity

This section analyzes enterprise performance in South Africa by examining several measures of productivity, including labor productivity, capital productivity, and total factor productivity. These measures are compared internationally and across different types of firms within South Africa.

Labor Productivity

Labor productivity is far higher in South Africa than elsewhere in Sub-Saharan Africa and even in other middle-income countries where Investment Climate Surveys have been completed (see figure 2.1). Labor productivity is more than four times higher for the median manufacturing

Figure 2.1 Cross-Country Comparison of Labor Productivity (in the Garment Industry)

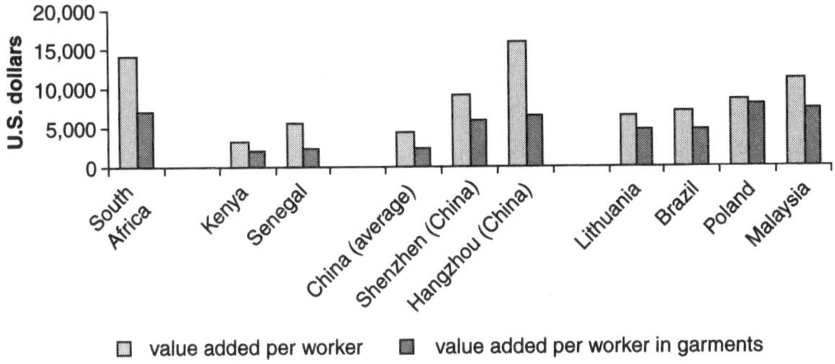

Source: Investment Climate Surveys.
Note: All values are medians for enterprises with available data. Value added is calculated by subtracting intermediate inputs and energy costs from sales from manufacturing. Workers include both permanent and temporary workers. Values are converted to U.S. dollars using average exchange rates for 2002 from *World Development Indicators*. Data are for 2002, except for Lithuania (2003).

firm in South Africa than for firms in Kenya and nearly three times higher for firms in Senegal. These two comparator countries were chosen because their labor (and total factor) productivity are high relative to other countries in Sub-Saharan Africa where Investment Climate Surveys have been completed, suggesting that the gap is large for most countries in Sub-Saharan Africa. These results are consistent with previous studies using aggregate data that have also found that productivity is higher in South Africa than elsewhere in Sub-Saharan Africa.[2]

Labor productivity in South Africa is also high compared with that in other middle-income countries where Investment Climate Surveys have been completed. Labor productivity is about twice as high in South Africa as in Brazil and Lithuania and is about 25 percent higher than in Malaysia. Labor productivity is also considerably higher than in China. Although China's per capita GDP is considerably lower than South Africa's, China has been growing rapidly since the late 1970s.

Although value added per worker is lower in China than in South Africa, interregional differences between Chinese cities and provinces are large; productivity is far higher in areas closer to the coast.[3] When South African firms are considered only in relation to firms in the most productive regions covered in the China ICS, the comparison is less favorable. Labor productivity is higher in South Africa than in Shenzhen, the second most productive city in the China ICS, but is slightly lower than in Hangzhou, the most productive city in the survey.

South African enterprises might be more productive than enterprises in other middle-income countries, because South African enterprises might be concentrated in industries that are especially capital, skill, or technology intensive. Over the 1980s and 1990s, South African manufacturing became increasingly capital intensive[4] due not only to firms' adoption of capital-intensive production methods but also to the expansion of manufacturing in capital-intensive sectors.[5]

To control for differences between sectors, figure 2.1 shows labor productivity in a single industry—the garment industry. This sector is chosen because the technologies are well established and because most ICSs have large numbers of garment manufacturers.

South African firms appear relatively productive in the garment industry, although the differences are less noticeable than they are for manufacturing overall. Labor productivity is higher for the median firm in the garments sector in South Africa than in Brazil and Lithuania but slightly lower than in Malaysia or Poland. Productivity is also higher than in either of the most productive cities in the China ICS.

South Africa appears worse in these comparisons because of the exchange rates used in the analysis. Exchange rate fluctuations can make a significant difference to labor productivity when converted to a common currency such as the U.S. dollar. In the year of the survey, the South African rand was very weak; the exchange rate averaged over 10 rand per dollar, potentially making value added per worker (and labor costs and capital intensity) appear artificially low. Between 2002 and 2004 the rand appreciated significantly in real terms, but this effect might have been muted by the appreciation of most currencies, with the notable exception of the Chinese yuan, against the U.S. dollar in real terms.[6]

Differences among South African firms are significant. In South Africa, as in most other countries, labor productivity is higher for exporters and foreign-owned enterprises than for other enterprises (table 2.2). Labor productivity is also notably higher in corporate-owned firms (that is, firms whose main owner is a domestic or foreign-owned enterprise rather than a family or individual). Differences among firms owned by white, Asian, and black or colored individuals and families are small.

In contrast to most other countries, where labor productivity increases with size, South Africa has no noticeable trend with respect to enterprise size. Although large firms appear more productive than small or medium-sized firms, they also appear more productive than very large firms. The latter might have low productivity, because they are in low productivity sectors. For example, about one-quarter of very large firms are in the

Table 2.2 Median Productivity by Industry, Size, Export Status, Location, and Ownership, 2002

	Capacity utilization	Capital per worker (book value, rand)	Capital productivity (book value)	Value added per worker (rand)	Labor cost per worker (rand)	Unit labor costs
Overall	***77.8***	***36,200***	***4.1***	***147,900***	***77,200***	***0.45***
Sector						
Garments	81.5	13,100	4.3	75,300	43,200	0.57
Food and beverage	77.0	30,900	4.0	210,300	63,000	0.28
Chemicals	72.3	52,900	4.0	218,800	98,900	0.41
Construction materials	86.2	49,300	4.5	99,500	96,000	0.28
Furniture and wood	77.7	26,700	5.2	114,100	53,800	0.48
Metals	78.9	39,100	4.5	151,500	94,300	0.54
Paper, publishing, and printing	78.5	40,100	3.2	166,000	71,100	0.47
Plastics	78.1	35,900	2.9	129,300	68,200	0.42
Machinery	74.8	37,100	7.7	198,800	96,500	0.51
Electrical equipment	79.2	32,700	4.9	183,300	74,600	0.44
Automobiles and auto parts	71.4	58,200	1.9	145,900	88,700	0.69
Other manufacturing	77.8	41,300	3.9	172,200	89,400	0.45
Size						
Small (10–49 employees)	75.6	45,400	3.2	122,300	63,700	0.45
Medium sized (50–99 employees)	79.5	43,500	3.1	125,800	73,900	0.54
Large (100–499 employees)	77.2	32,000	6.3	201,300	88,800	0.41
Very large (over 500 employees)	80.2	34,800	4.5	140,700	79,700	0.44
Export status						
Nonexporters	77.9	35,100	4.1	132,000	70,700	0.46
Exporters	77.6	40,300	4.2	187,000	89,500	0.44
Foreign ownership						
Domestically owned	77.9	34,800	4.0	135,000	71,700	0.48
Foreign owned	77.3	40,900	4.3	222,200	98,600	0.37
Province						
Gauteng	77.4	40,100	4.2	174,700	91,600	0.50
KwaZulu-Natal	81.4	23,500	3.8	113,900	48,800	0.36
Western Cape	77.6	26,300	4.4	91,800	42,700	0.40
Eastern Cape	76.1	54,900	4.1	145,900	66,800	0.44
Ownership						
Corporate owned	77.3	43,000	4.4	213,400	98,700	0.39
Individual/family—black/colored	71.5	27,700	4.2	112,400	67,600	0.55
Individual/family—European/Caucasian	79.1	30,000	4.0	119,400	59,900	0.52
Individual/family—Asian	76.0	38,300	3.3	105,700	58,100	0.49

Source: Investment Climate Survey.

Note: See figures in this chapter for detailed notes. Workers are permanent and temporary workers. Capital is the book value of machinery and equipment. All numbers are medians, except for capacity utilization, which is a mean.

garment industry—a sector with especially low labor productivity. After controlling for sectoral differences, labor productivity is not significantly different in large firms and very large firms.[7]

Although labor productivity is relatively high in South Africa, labor costs are also high when calculated with data from firms' income statements (see figure 2.2). The total cost of wages and other benefits is higher per worker in South Africa than in any of the comparator countries. In 2002 per worker labor costs were over three and half times higher in South Africa (about $7,300 per worker) than in Hangzhou (about $2,000 per worker). Differences in the textiles and garment industries are smaller than overall differences; in this sector, per worker labor costs in Malaysia and Poland come close to those in South Africa.

Because per worker labor costs are high, unit labor costs (that is, labor costs as a share of value added) are higher in South Africa than they are in China, Kenya, or Senegal (figure 2.3). South Africa has unit labor costs slightly higher than those in Brazil and Malaysia and slightly lower than those in the two countries in Eastern Europe.

For cross-country comparisons, unit labor costs have several advantages over comparisons of per worker labor costs in a common currency. First, they avoid problems associated with exchange rate fluctuations, because both labor costs and value added are measured in local currency. Second, they partially account for differences in skills. For example, both labor productivity and labor costs will appear high if a firm has a highly

Figure 2.2 Cross-Country Comparison of Labor Costs

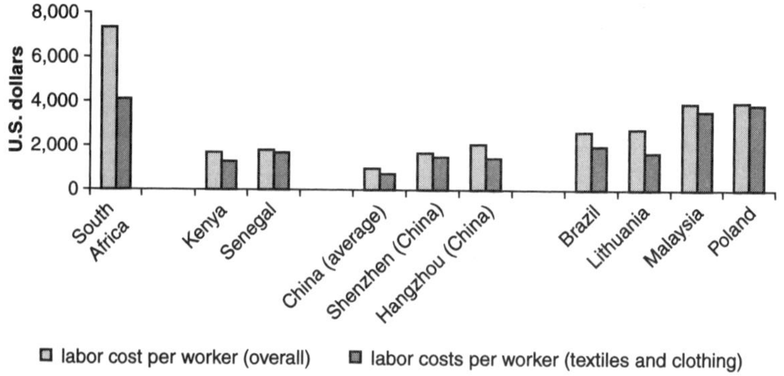

Source: Investment Climate Surveys.

Note: All values are medians for enterprises with available data. Values are converted to U.S. dollars using average exchange rates for 2002 from *World Development Indicators*. Labor cost is the total cost of wages and salaries and allowances, bonuses, and other benefits for both production and administrative staff.

Figure 2.3 Cross-Country Comparison of Unit Labor Costs

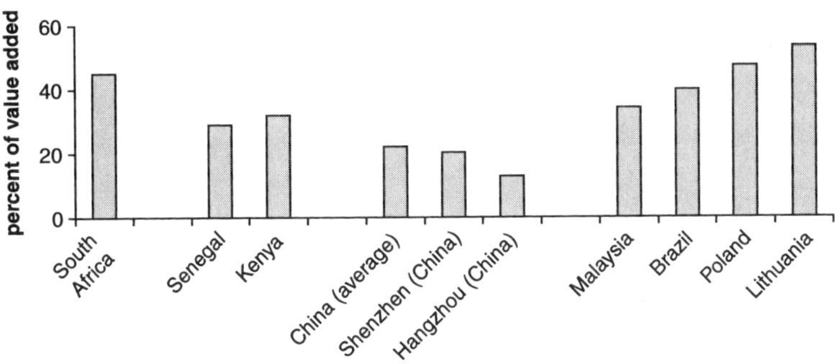

Source: Investment Climate Surveys.
Note: All values are medians for enterprises with available data. Value added is calculated by subtracting intermediate inputs and energy costs from sales from manufacturing. Values are converted to U.S. dollars using average exchange rates for 2002 from *World Development Indicators*. Labor cost is the total cost of wages and salaries and allowances, bonuses, and other benefits for both production and administrative staff.

educated workforce. Overall, these results suggest that labor costs are relatively high in South Africa—at least relative to Asia, Latin America, and elsewhere in Sub-Saharan Africa—even after taking South Africa's higher productivity into account. Chapter 3 explores these issues in more detail.

Labor costs tend to be higher for firms that are more productive at the firm level. The simple correlation between labor costs per worker and value added per worker is 0.46 (significant at a 1 percent level). A similar pattern can be seen at an aggregate level in table 2.2. Labor costs and productivity are higher in exporters, foreign-owned firms, firms located in Gauteng province, and corporate-owned firms than in other firms. As with labor productivity, no clear pattern for labor costs by firm size emerges. Although labor costs per worker are lower for small and medium-size firms than for large and very large firms, labor costs are higher for large firms than for very large firms.

Capital Productivity

Enterprises in South Africa appear to be more capital intensive than enterprises in most of the comparator countries (figure 2.4). Given average exchange rates in 2002, the median enterprise in South Africa had almost twice as much capital as the median enterprise in Shenzhen and Hangzhou and more than twice as much as in Lithuania and Brazil. Malaysian and Polish firms had slightly more capital per worker than South African firms. Given that the rand was weak in 2002 relative to the Polish zloty and the U.S. dollar, these comparisons might underestimate the amount of capital per worker in South Africa.[8]

Despite being highly capital intensive (even compared with firms in other middle-income countries), South African firms' capital productivity (value added over capital) remains relatively high. Although this capital productivity is lower than that of Brazil, Lithuania, and the most productive provinces in China—enterprises were considerably less capital intensive in these countries than in South Africa—it remains higher than that of Malaysia, Poland, or the rest of China.

In South Africa, as in other countries, exporters and foreign-owned enterprises appear more capital intensive than other enterprises, although the difference is modest. But in South Africa, in sharp contrast to most other countries, small enterprises appear more capital intensive than larger enterprises. In part, this difference might reflect sectoral differences. For example, garment firms are far less capital intensive than other firms and tend to be very large. After controlling for sector of operations, enterprises in the different size classes appear similar.[9]

Enterprises owned by black individuals appear to have less capital per worker than firms owned by white or Asian individuals. The difference, however, is not large and does not appear to be statistically significant, especially after controlling for other differences (for example, sector of operations and size).

Figure 2.4 Cross-Country Comparison of Capital Intensity

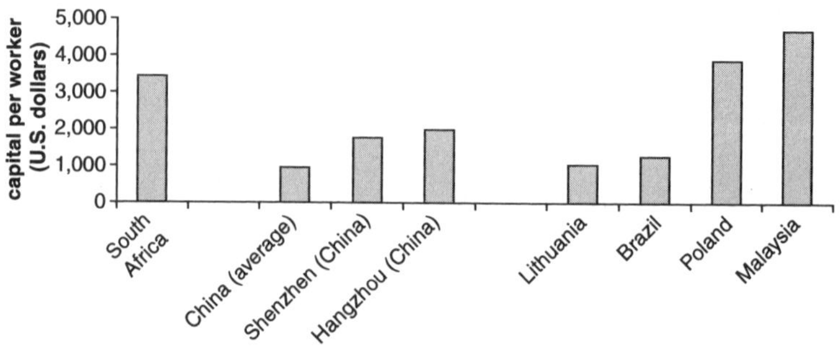

Source: Investment Climate Surveys.

Note: All values are medians for all enterprises with available data. Capital is the net book value of machinery and equipment at the end of 2002. Workers include both permanent and temporary workers. Values are converted to U.S. dollars using average exchange rates for 2002 from *World Development Indicators*.

Figure 2.5 Cross-Country Comparison of Capital Productivity

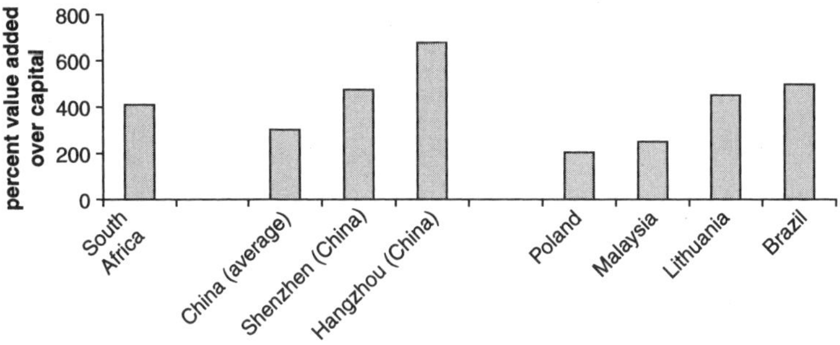

Source: Investment Climate Surveys.
Note: All values are medians for enterprises with available data. Value added is calculated by subtracting intermediate inputs and energy costs from sales from manufacturing. Capital is the net book value of machinery and equipment at the end of 2002.

Capacity Utilization

The survey asked enterprise managers to estimate capacity utilization—how large their firms' actual production was in 2002 relative to the maximum amount that could have been produced with the capital and workers employed at that time. The average enterprise in South Africa reported that its capacity utilization was about 78 percent (figure 2.6)—considerably higher than in most other African countries—including Kenya, Tanazania, and Uganda (60 percent) and Mali and Senegal (about 70 percent)—and higher than the average for China (about 70 percent). But capacity utilization in South Africa was lower than that in the best-performing middle-income comparator countries and in the most productive provinces in China.

In South Africa, capacity utilization varies little by enterprise size or other characteristics; it mostly averages between 75 and 80 percent. In 2002 capacity utilization was highest in the construction materials and garments sectors and lowest in the automobiles and auto parts sectors.

Total Factor Productivity

Although the measures of firm productivity discussed above provide some useful information on firm performance in South Africa, they can be misleading when considered in isolation. Total factor productivity (TFP) is a measure of the overall level of firm performance after controlling for use of labor and capital. Differences in TFP are those differences in output that cannot be explained by differences in the amounts of

Figure 2.6 Cross-Country Comparison of Capacity Utilization

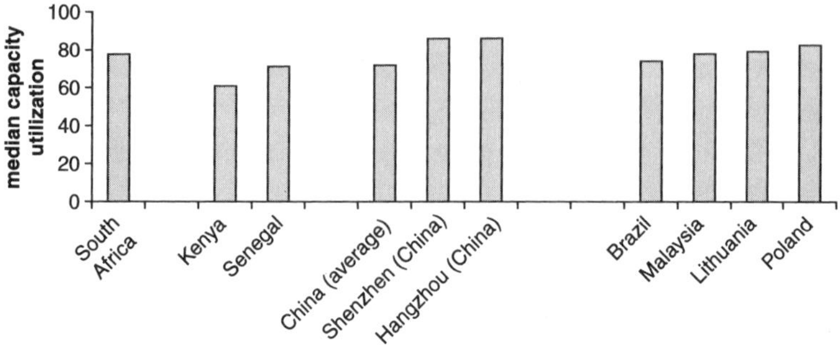

Source: Investment Climate Surveys.
Note: Data for all countries is for 2002. All values are medians for enterprises with available data. Capacity utilization is directly reported by enterprise managers and is defined as the amount of output that is actually produced relative to the maximum amount that could be produced given current capital stock and employment.

labor, capital, or intermediate inputs used. Firms with higher TFP are more efficient than other firms, because they produce higher output with fewer inputs.

Table 2.3 presents results from estimating a Cobb-Douglas production function using data for South African enterprises from all manufacturing subsectors. The production function is estimated by using a standard stochastic frontier approach, which allows technical efficiency (how well the individual firm performs relative to the best firms in the sample) to be distinguished from random noise (due to shocks or measurement error).[10]

Sector-Specific Production Technologies—The dependent variable is the natural log of value added, and all regressions control for the enterprises' use of capital and workers.[11] All regressions include sector dummies, allowing average productivity to differ among sectors. Because enterprises in different sectors use different production technologies, the coefficients on labor and capital are likely to differ among sectors. Therefore, the sector dummies are interacted with capital and labor, allowing sector-specific production technologies.[12] A joint test of the significance of the interaction terms rejects the null hypothesis that the coefficients are equal across sectors. Therefore, pooling enterprises from different sectors into a single model without controlling for sector differences related to factor intensity would be inappropriate.

Economies of Scale—If large enterprises were consistently more productive than small enterprises, the sum of the coefficients on intermediate

Table 2.3 Impact of Enterprise Characteristics on Total Factor Productivity

	Value added (natural log)							
Observations	*486*	*485*	*484*	*485*	*411*	*465*	*485*	*410*
Production function								
Capital (sales value)	0.4653***	0.4819***	0.4726***	0.4299***	0.4729***	0.4933***	0.4906***	0.4331***
(natural log)	(4.97)	(5.49)	(5.56)	(5.02)	(4.13)	(5.12)	(5.60)	(3.93)
Workers	0.5857***	0.4881***	0.4873***	0.5585***	0.5021***	0.4949***	0.4824***	0.5553***
(natural log)	(5.01)	(4.45)	(4.61)	(5.30)	(3.25)	(4.08)	(4.43)	(3.78)
Enterprise characteristics								
Age of enterprise		0.0961***	0.1030***	0.0819**	0.0802**	0.0885***	0.0970***	0.0756**
(natural log of years)		(2.84)	(3.13)	(2.52)	(2.26)	(2.62)	(2.88)	(2.25)
Enterprise is partially government owned		−1.0396**	−1.2660***	−1.3822***	−2.1037***	−0.9992*	−1.1067**	−2.0705***
(dummy)		(2.01)	(2.64)	(2.89)	(3.24)	(1.95)	(2.14)	(3.40)
Enterprise owner—corporation		0.5971***	0.5628***	0.5480***	0.6318***	0.6030***	0.5567***	0.5977***
(dummy)		(3.93)	(3.72)	(3.74)	(3.92)	(3.91)	(3.65)	(3.80)
Enterprise owners—Caucasian/ European family/individual		0.1804	0.1790	0.2014	0.2460	0.1916	0.1705	0.2823*
(dummy)		(1.21)	(1.23)	(1.40)	(1.55)	(1.26)	(1.15)	(1.86)
Enterprise owner—Asian family/individual		0.0079	0.0381	0.0819	0.0737	0.0257	−0.0193	0.1727
(dummy)		(0.04)	(0.21)	(0.45)	(0.38)	(0.14)	(0.10)	(0.92)
Globalization								
Exports			0.0065***					0.0061***
(as % of sales)			(4.23)					(3.78)
Enterprise is partially foreign owned			0.0741					0.0375
(dummy)			(0.85)					(0.40)

(continued)

Table 2.3 Impact of Enterprise Characteristics on Total Factor Productivity *(continued)*

	Value added (natural log)							
Observations	*486*	*485*	*484*	*485*	*411*	*465*	*485*	*410*
Technology use								
Percent of workers using computers				0.0097***				0.0075***
				(6.16)				(4.45)
Human capital								
Manager has tertiary education					0.2493**			0.2022**
(dummy)					(2.56)			(2.16)
Percent of workers with primary education					–0.0067**			–0.0036
(dummy)					(2.27)			(1.27)
Percent of workers with secondary education					–0.0075***			–0.0033
(dummy)					(2.77)			(1.24)
Training								
Percent of unskilled workers						–0.0007		
who received formal training						(0.47)		
Percent of skilled workers						0.0016		
who received formal training						(1.13)		
Access to capital								
Firm has overdraft facility							–0.1237*	
(dummy)							(1.80)	
Firm has bank loan							–0.0520	
(dummy)							(0.81)	

Source: Authors' calculations using Investment Climate Survey.

Notes: T-statistics are in parentheses. The dependent variable is a log of value added. Capital is the amount the enterprise would receive if it sold its capital.

*** Significant at 1 percent level; ** significant at 5 percent level; * significant at 10 percent level.

Coefficients are reported for firms in the agro-industry sector. In addition, sector dummies and sector-specific production functions are included for 12 sectors (agro-industry; chemicals and paints; construction materials; metals; furniture and wood; paper, printing, and publishing; plastic; machinery; auto and auto parts; electrical goods; other manufacturing; and textiles, garments, and leather). The dummies are interacted with capital, labor, and intermediate inputs to allow sector-specific production technologies.

inputs, labor, and capital would be greater than one. In that case, total production would more than double if the number of workers and the amount of capital were doubled. In practice, the sum of the coefficients is very close to one for all sectors, with the exception of garments and construction materials (table 2.4). Further, the null hypothesis that the coefficients add up to one cannot be rejected for any of the sectors except garments at conventional significance levels. By implication, large enterprises are neither more nor less productive than small enterprises on average.

Other Enterprise Characteristics—In addition to capital and labor, other enterprise characteristics affect total factor productivity. Enterprises that are younger, partially government-owned, and owned by individuals or families (rather than other firms) tend to be less productive than other enterprises.

The coefficient on government ownership is negative and statistically significant. The coefficient estimate suggests that government-owned firms are about 120 to 200 percent less productive than similar privately owned firms. But this finding must be interpreted with caution. Only four firms in the sample are even partially government owned, meaning that the results are based on a very small number of observations.

Older firms are also more productive. The positive and statistically significant coefficient suggests that a 10 percent increase in age increases output by about 1 percent. On the basis of these coefficients, a firm that

Table 2.4 Test for Constant Returns to Scale

	Sum of coefficients	*Test of constant returns to scale*	
		F-value	*p-value*
Agro-processing	0.99	0.03	0.86
Textiles and garments	0.72	13.41	0.00
Chemicals and paints	1.04	0.25	0.61
Construction materials	1.42	2.72	0.10
Furniture	1.04	0.23	0.63
Metal	1.02	0.07	0.78
Paper, publishing, and printing	0.87	2.03	0.15
Plastics	1.10	0.84	0.36
Machinery	1.23	2.53	0.11
Electricity	1.13	2.13	0.14
Auto and auto parts	0.99	0.00	0.95
Other manufacturing	0.87	2.36	0.12

Source: Authors' calculations using Investment Climate Survey.
Note: Coefficient estimates are from column 8 of table 2.3.

began operating in 1990 would be between 10 and 12 percent more efficient than a similar firm that began operating in 2000.

The positive and statistically significant coefficient on the dummy, indicating that the firm is owned by another firm, suggests that corporate-owned firms are about 60 percent more productive than firms owned by black or colored families or individuals (the omitted category). Because the coefficients on the other dummy variables are statistically insignificant in most specifications, corporate-owned firms would appear to be more productive than firms owned by all types of individuals or families. No evidence was found that differences among different types of family- and individually owned firms are statistically significant.

Globalization—In column 3 of table 2.3, some additional variables—the percent of output that the firm exports and a dummy variable indicating whether the enterprise is foreign owned—are added to the model. The coefficient on the dummy variable indicating that the enterprise is partly foreign owned is positive but statistically insignificant. Results are similar when majority-owned foreign firms and corporate-owned foreign firms, rather than all firms with any foreign ownership, are examined.

The positive coefficient on share of output that is exported is positive and statistically significant, suggesting that enterprises that export more intensively are more productive. On the basis of the coefficient estimates, firms that export 37 percent of their output (the mean for enterprises that export) will be about 22 to 24 percent more productive than firms that export none of their output. Many studies have found similar results in both developed and developing economies.[13]

Exporting might result in productivity improvements for the firms engaged in it (the "learning-by-exporting" hypothesis). The discipline of competing in international markets might encourage enterprises to improve their productivity or might expose them to foreign technologies or modes of production. But consider an alternate hypothesis. Because firms have to be efficient to compete in international markets, only firms that are already efficient are able to export (the "self-selectivity" hypothesis). Although inefficient firms might be protected from international competition in domestic markets by natural barriers (for example, high transportation costs) and policy barriers to trade (for example, government tariffs and quotas or inefficient ports or customs administration), they are unable to enter international markets.

The above hypotheses are not mutually exclusive. Even if efficient firms are more likely to start exporting, that activity could help them further increase their productivity.[14] The results from this study cannot support one of the two hypotheses over the other.

Technology—In column 4 of table 2.3, a variable representing information and communication technology (ICT) use—the percent of workers that use computers for their work—is included in the model. The coefficient on this variable is positive and statistically significant, suggesting that firms that use ICT more intensively are more productive than enterprises that do not. A one percentage point increase in the share of workers using computers increases productivity by between three-quarters and one percent.

Consider an additional ICT-related measure: a dummy variable indicating that the firm uses e-mail to communicate with clients and suppliers. In other countries in Africa, firms that do so appear more productive than those that do not. When this variable is included in the analysis for South Africa, the coefficient is statistically insignificant with a negative coefficient. E-mail appears less important in South Africa than in other countries in Sub-Saharan Africa, because over 98 percent of South African enterprises use it, meaning that variation along this dimension is small.

Human Capital—In column 5 of table 2.3, several additional variables representing the firm's human capital are added to the base regression. The variables are a dummy variable indicating that the firm's manager has a graduate (bachelor of arts, bachelor of science, and so on) or higher degree. In addition, the regression includes two variables indicating the percent of employees who have fewer than 6 years of education and the percent of employees who have between 6 and 12 years of education.

Managerial and worker education both affect productivity. Firms with a manager who holds a graduate degree are between 20 and 25 percent more productive than firms with less educated managers. Worker education also matters; firms with more employees possessing some tertiary education are more productive than firms with more employees possessing only primary or secondary education. The coefficients on the two variables suggest that increasing the education of employees with a primary education or less to a secondary education would not have a large impact on productivity, because the coefficients are almost identical. In fact, tests fail to reject the null hypothesis that the coefficients are equal, suggesting that the main difference is between firms with more employees possessing a tertiary education and firms with employees possessing only primary and secondary education. The results for worker education are not highly robust. When they are included, along with the other variables with statistically significant coefficients (see column 8), their coefficients become smaller and statistically insignificant.

Training—In column 6 of table 2.3, two variables related to firms' training programs—the percent of skilled workers and the percent of unskilled workers who received formal training in that year—are added to the base regression. The coefficients on the two variables are small and statistically insignificant at conventional significance levels. The coefficient on percent of unskilled workers who received training was negative, although statistically significant. As a robustness check, these variables were replaced with a simple dummy variable indicating that the firm offered a formal training program to its employees. The coefficient on this variable was also statistically insignificant with a small negative sign.

One possible explanation for this finding is that firms may be more likely to have formal training programs for workers when they have a high number of new, poorly educated, or inexperienced employees. The result, however, suggests that training programs, as currently designed, might not be fulfilling their desired purpose.

Access to Finance—As a final exercise, two dummy variables indicating that the firms have overdraft facilities and bank loans are added to the base regression. The coefficients on these variables are both negative. And the coefficient on the dummy indicating that the firm has an overdraft facility is marginally statistically significant. The negative coefficient suggests that firms with overdraft facilities are about 12 percent less efficient than other enterprises.

If firms were starved for credit, the coefficient on this variable would be expected to be positive. If banks make few loans, better firms would be expected to be more likely to get them. Even if banks were doing a poor job of allocating credit to the most productive firms, a positive coefficient would still be expected if lack of credit was hurting the performance of firms without access.

One plausible explanation for the negative coefficient is that better-performing firms have less need of bank credit. That is, the most efficient firms—which should be more profitable than less efficient firms, all other factors equal—are better able to finance investment and working capital from retained earnings and might have better access to other sources of credit (for example, equity or trade credit). Thus, firms with bank credit appear less, not more, productive than firms without such credit.

In summary, firms that are older, are completely privately owned, export more, use technology more intensively, and have better educated managers and workers tend to be more efficient. But evidence that firms with training programs are more efficient is lacking. This final result could be explained in two ways: firms with poorer-quality workers have to train them more intensively, or current training programs are ineffective.

Profitability

At the enterprise level, profitability is associated with better firm performance. Firms that are more productive and have lower overhead costs will be more profitable than other firms.[15] But at the industry level, high profitability could also reflect a lack of competition. Firms will be able to earn higher profits in less competitive markets than in more competitive markets, where profits typically will be competed away.

Macroeconomic evidence suggests that profits declined significantly before 1994 but that they have risen significantly since then. Overall, the net rate of profit in the private sector was two-thirds higher in 2001 than in 1990 (Nattrass 2003, 148). The only sector that saw a small decline in the net profit rate was manufacturing—one of the three sectors covered in this Investment Climate Survey. The major increases in profits occurred in trade, catering, and accommodation and in finance and business services. With the highest rates of return, these sectors have been growing most rapidly; consequently, the sectoral composition of the economy will continue to change.

For the median manufacturing enterprise in the South Africa ICS that was operating only in domestic markets, profitability was about 7.0 percent in 2002 (figure 2.7), slightly higher than that of firms in Malaysia (6.5 percent) and slightly lower than that of firms in Brazil (16.1 percent).[16] Because indirect costs and depreciation were unavailable for surveyed firms in Lithuania and Poland, profitability is calculated in a different way for all five middle-income comparator countries without excluding these items. The results for Brazil, Malaysia, and South Africa were qualitatively similar. Profitability was lower in South Africa than in Brazil—although the difference was closer than before—and higher than in Malaysia. Profitability was higher in South Africa than in Lithuania and Poland.

Given that industrial concentration is thought to be exceptionally high in South Africa, it might appear strange that profitability, while high, is not completely out of line with profitability in the other middle-income countries where ICSs have been completed. Two explanations

Figure 2.7 Cross-Country Comparison of Profitability

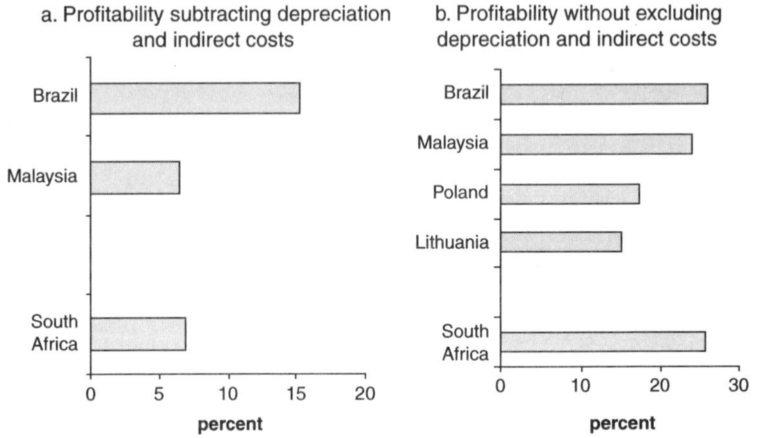

Source: Investment Climate Surveys.
Note: Profitability is calculated by subtracting wages and other labor costs, the cost of intermediate inputs, indirect costs, and depreciation of capital from sales and dividing by sales. Exporting firms are excluded to catch profitability in domestic markets.

are plausible. First, although market concentration might result in excess profits, other stakeholders might capture them. Consistent with this idea, Fedderke and Szalontai (2005) find that unit labor costs are higher in South African industries that are more highly concentrated. If labor successfully captures a portion of the excess profits, market concentration might not lead to large increases in profitability. Second, this result appears to be broadly consistent with research on price markups in different countries. In particular, one study found that markups in South Africa appeared to fall within the range of those estimated for other countries in international studies.[17]

Exporting

About 34 percent of South African firms exported at least 10 percent of their output in 2002. The average firm exported about 14 percent of sales (figure 2.8)—more than the average firm in Brazil and Poland (7 and 10 percent of sales) but less than the average firm in Lithuania (28 percent of sales).

South African manufacturing firms lagged behind Malaysia and the best-performing provinces in China in this respect. Only 15 percent of Chinese firms were involved in exporting; the average firm exported 11 percent of sales, primarily due to the low export performance of firms

Figure 2.8 Cross-Country Comparison of Exports

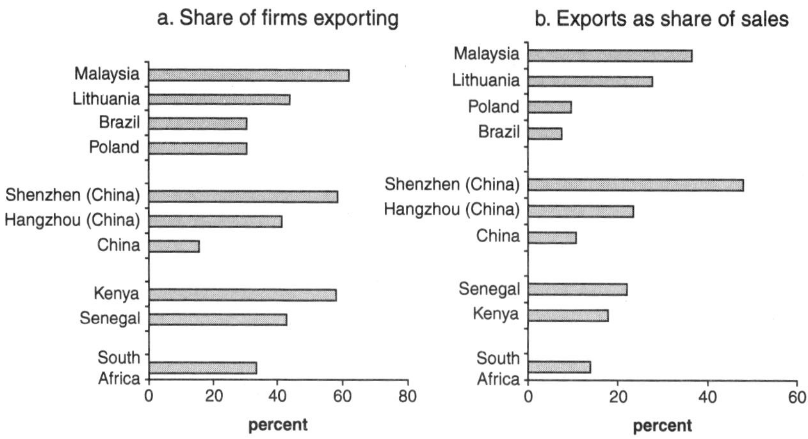

Source: Investment Climate Surveys.
Note: Firms are considered to be exporters when they export at least 10 percent of their output.

in interior provinces. In the most productive provinces included in the survey, Chinese firms were more likely to export than South African firms (42 percent in Hangzhou and 58 percent in Shenzhen), and the average firm in these provinces exported more of its output than the average firm in South Africa (23 percent in Hangzhou and 48 percent in Shenzhen). Malaysian firms were also more likely to export, and they exported a greater share of sales than firms in South Africa.

Although South African firms were less likely to export than firms in Kenya and Senegal, these two countries considerably outperformed the other countries in Sub-Saharan Africa where ICSs have been completed. For example, only 26 percent of Tanzanian firms, 19 percent of Ugandan firms, and 7 percent of Ethiopian firms exported any part of their production.

Exports from South African firms differ from exports from other African firms in another way. South African exporters were more likely to export outside of Africa (table 2.5). Firms in the surveys were asked to list their three most important export partners. Kenyan firms' top three export destinations were Uganda (74 percent), Tanzania (61 percent), and Rwanda (19 percent); among industrialized countries, Kenyan firms' top export destination was the United Kingdom (8 percent). A similar pattern emerged in Senegal, where the top three destinations were all neighboring countries in West Africa.

In contrast, 24 percent of South African firms included the United Kingdom among their top three destinations and 20 percent included the

Table 2.5 Main Export Destinations for Enterprises in the Investment Climate Surveys

	Most important export destinations (percent of exporters that report destination is important)	*Most important industrialized export destination (percent of exporters that report destination is most important destination)*
South Africa	United Kingdom (24); United States (20); Namibia (19)	United Kingdom (24)
Kenya	Uganda (74); Tanzania (61); Rwanda (19)	United Kingdom (8)
Senegal	Gambia (39); Mali (36); Mauritania (31)	France (18)
China	United States (32); Japan (31); Germany (10); Korea (10)	United States (32)

Source: Investment Climate Surveys.
Note: Countries are ranked on the basis of the number of enterprises that ranked them among their top three export destinations. Not all enterprises reported three destinations.

United States. The top African destination was Namibia, which 19 percent of firms included in their top three destinations. In this respect, South Africa is more like China, where the top three destinations were the United States, Japan, and Germany.

About 55 percent of South African enterprises included at least one African country among their top three export partners, whereas about 57 percent included at least one non-African country in their top three. Most firms, however, included only either African countries or non-African countries among the top three—few counted both African and non-African firms among their top export destinations. Although 34 percent of exporters reported at least one Southern African Customs Union (SACU) country among their top three export destinations and 50 percent reported at least one non-SACU country among their top three, only 2 percent of firms that included an Organisation of Economic Co-operation and Development (OECD) member country among their top destinations also included an African country in SACU among their top three and only 17 percent included an African country not in SACU (see table 2.6). In contrast, 56 percent of firms that included an African country not in SACU among their top three destinations also included an African country in SACU.

Exports in South Africa increased as a percent of sales between 2000 and 2002. The average firm exported about 12 percent of sales in 2000 and about 14 percent of sales in 2002. The share of firms involved in exporting also increased—from 30 percent in 2000 to 34 percent in 2002. This increase might suggest that South African firms have become more competitive, but note that the rand depreciated by about 24 percent in real terms over this period and depreciated by slightly more against the U.S. dollar, the euro, and the British pound (about 26 to 28 percent).[18]

Table 2.6 Export Destinations
(percent)

	All exporters	*With OECD country in top 3*	*With SACU country in top 3*	*With non-SACU African country in top 3*	*With other country in top 3*
With OECD countries among top 3 destinations	51	—	3	18	70
With SACU countries among top 3	34	2	—	56	12
With non-SACU African countries among top 3	50	17	84	—	30
With non-African/non-OECD countries among top 3	20	27	7	12	—
With only non-African countries among top 3	44	—	—	—	—
With only African countries among top 3	42	—	—	—	—
With both African and non-African countries in top 3	13	—	—	—	—

Source: Investment Climate Surveys.
Note: Enterprises are classified on the basis of countries listed among their top three export destinations. Not all enterprises reported three destinations.

Because this depreciation makes South African goods relatively cheaper in dollar terms, exporting might be expected to increase.

When calculated in rand, export growth appeared relatively robust over this period, increasing by about 21 percent for the average firm and about 24 percent for the median firm in the survey (figure 2.9). Growth was especially robust for firms that exported primarily to OECD economies and outside of SACU. Among firms that exported primarily to OECD economies, exports for the average firm grew by 38 percent and for the median firm by 34 percent. Among firms that primarily exported to other countries in SACU, exports grew more slowly when measured in rand (7 percent for the median firm and 21 percent for the average firm). Because the currencies of most other countries in SACU are pegged to the rand, the increase was more modest.

Due to the depreciation of the rand, export growth might be overstated when measured in rand. Studies using aggregate data suggest that South African firms are price takers in international markets (Edwards 2005). Therefore, measurement in dollar terms might be the most appropriate way of measuring export growth at the firm level, at least for firms exporting to OECD economies.[19] Measured in dollar terms, exports

Figure 2.9 Average Export Growth, 2000 and 2002

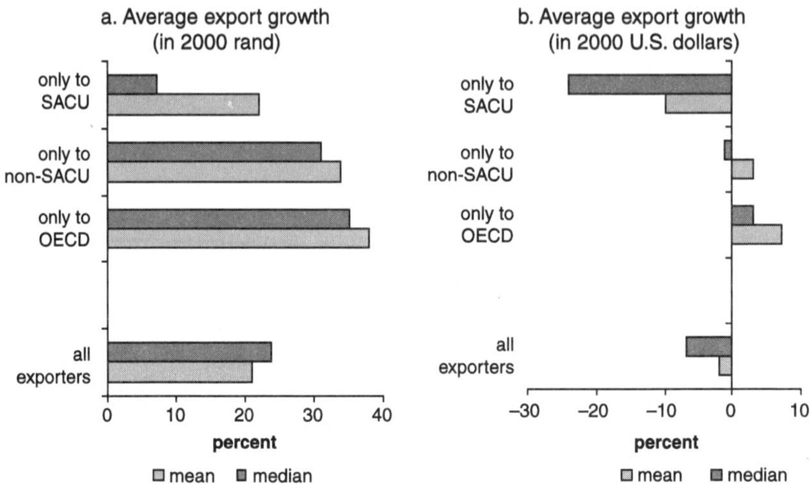

Source: Investment Climate Surveys.
Note: Average export growth rates for all exporters include all firms that export. Average growth rates for exporters that export only to Southern African Customs Union are average rates for firms that report only SACU countries among their top three export destinations. Rates for exporters that export only to non-SACU and Organisation of Economic Co-operation and Development economies are defined similarly.

actually fell between 2000 and 2002—7 percent for the median firm and 2 percent for the mean firm. Among firms that primarily export to OECD economies, exports increased slightly in dollar terms—3 percent for the median firm and 7 percent on average.

The modest short-run export supply response might appear inconsistent with macroeconomic evidence that suggests a relatively large long-run response. For example, Edwards (2005) finds that a 1 percent increase in the relative price of exports raises average manufacturing exports by between 1.8 and 2.5 percent, whereas Edwards and Golub (2004) find a long-run elasticity of between 1.6 and 2.8 percent. However, short-run export responses appear to be considerably smaller than long-run responses. Edwards (2005) estimates that a 1 percent increase in relative prices increased exports by 0.3 to 0.4 percent in the short run during the 1980s and 1990s—a more appropriate comparator for these figures. Furthermore, previous work using firm-level data from the Greater Johannesburg Metropolitan Area has suggested that exports by small and medium-size South African manufacturers (those with less than 200 employees) responded only modestly to changes in the real exchange rate in the 1990s (Chandra and others 2001b). The modest response to changes in the real exchange rate might be due to risk aversion: 30 percent of the small and medium-size firms in the previous study decided to wait and see whether the depreciation would be reversed before they altered production plans or moved away from imports. Because the ICS is made up predominantly of small and medium-size enterprises—over half the firms have fewer than 100 employees and nearly three-quarters have fewer than 200 employees—the response by these enterprises has not surprisingly been modest.

Notes

1. The report focuses on manufacturing, presenting evidence from other sectors primarily when results differ across sectors.
2. Edwards and Golub (2003) show that productivity was over 50 percent higher in South Africa than in Zimbabwe in 1997, while Mbaye and Golub (2003) show that productivity was about two and half times higher than in Senegal in 1996.
3. Dollar and others (2005) discuss regional differences in the investment climate and productivity of China.
4. Fedderke (2005) notes that most of the increase in manufacturing output over the past 30 years appears to be attributable to increased use of capital, a phenomenon consistent with the observation that output has become more capital intensive in recent years. Many papers have noted that South African manufacturing appears to have become more capital intensive over the past several decades (Edwards and Golub 2003; Levy 1992). Finally, several studies of trading patterns have noted that industry in South Africa tends to be more capital intensive than industry in South Africa's main trading partners.
5. Kaplinsky (1995) argues that in the 1980s this expansion was due to expansion in capital-intensive sectors and contraction in labor-intensive ones.
6. In April 2002, one U.S. dollar was worth about 11.4 rand. By April 2005, it was worth about 6.2 rand. But the same decline was far less pronounced against the euro, which declined from 10.0 rand to about 8.0 rand per euro.
7. When labor productivity is regressed on size and sector dummies, the null hypothesis that labor productivity is equal for large and very large enterprises cannot be rejected at conventional significance levels.
8. There were 2.75 rand per zloty in April 2002, compared with 1.97 in April 2005.
9. In a regression of capital intensity on a series of sector and size dummies, the null hypothesis that the coefficients on the size dummies are all equal cannot be rejected.
10. See Kumbhakar and Lovell (2000) for a description of stochastic frontier models. The model estimated assumes that the technical inefficiency component

is distributed with a half-normal distribution, while the white noise component is distributed with a normal distribution. In practice, the results discussed in this section appear to be relatively robust to alternate distributional assumptions (for example, truncated normal-normal distributions and exponential-normal distributions). Results are similar when the model is estimated using different modeling assumptions [for example, ordinary least squares (OLS) and least absolute deviation (LAD) estimators].

11. Results are similar when using log of sales as the dependent variable and including intermediate inputs, along with labor and capital, as an input.

12. Formally, the coefficients on capital and labor are allowed to vary across sectors. This system is estimated by interacting sector dummies with these variables. The model is estimated after adding the sector dummies and interaction terms to the regression. These coefficients are not reported in the table due to space constraints.

13. Tybout (2003) and Keller (2003) summarize the literature on this topic.

14. The evidence appears to support both hypotheses to some degree. For example, several econometric studies that examined whether enterprises improve their productivity before or after they start exporting have found that productivity improvements precede exporting, providing support for the self-selectivity hypothesis [see, for example, Clerides, Lach, and Tybout (1998); Bernard and Jensen (1999); Liu, Tsou, and Hammitt (1999); Aw, Chung, and Roberts (2000)]. However, case studies often support the "learning by exporting" hypothesis. Studies of exporters in Korea and Taiwan found that export buyers were an important source for new technologies, which they provided in various forms, including complete blueprints, information about manufacturing processes and quality control methods, technical advice and onsite plant inspections, and training for technical and production staff (Westphal 2002).

15. This is true in this data set. The simple correlation between technical efficiency and profitability is 0.16 and is statistically significant at a 1 percent level. This remains true after controlling for enterprise size, sector, and age.

16. Due to data considerations, profitability is defined differently from in the macroeconomic series. Profitability is calculated by subtracting wages and other labor costs, the cost of intermediate inputs, indirect costs, and depreciation of capital from sales and dividing by sales.

17. See Edwards and van de Winkel (2005). When intermediate inputs were excluded, markups appeared to be in the lower end of the range; when included, markups were in the higher end of the range. A separate study (Fedderke, Kularatne, and Mariotti 2003) found higher markups when excluding intermediate inputs and lower markups when including them. However, the markups from also fell within the range estimated in international studies (Hoekman, Kee, and Olarreaga 2001; Kee and Hoekman 2003).

18. The trade-weighted real exchange rate is from the International Monetary Fund (IMF 2005). The bilateral exchange rates are calculated with the formula from Hinkle and Montiel (1999, 45), using the Consumer Price Index as measure of inflation.
19. If South African firms make up a relatively small share of the market in most of these manufactured goods, international prices (measured in dollars or euros) might not change significantly due to the depreciation of the rand. That is, if South African exporters set prices and earn revenues in dollars or euros, revenue will increase in rand due to depreciation, even if firms do not export greater quantities. Estimating export revenues in dollars is likely to underestimate growth in exports to countries such as the SACU economies that peg their currency to the rand.

CHAPTER 3

Characteristics of the Labor Market

A well-functioning labor market is vital to the success of the government's policies to redress historical inequalities and establish a vibrant and globally competitive economy. This goal is an integral part of the government's Growth, Employment and Redistribution program (Government of South Africa 1996).

This chapter presents firm-level data provided by the personnel managers of surveyed firms together with individual-level employee survey data as a basis for a detailed description of the labor market in the manufacturing, construction, and retail sectors. It begins with a broad description of the labor market in these sectors and examines wage-setting behavior, worker training, and the determinants of employment growth. It concludes with information on labor regulations in South Africa.

The manufacturing sector accounts for 18.4 percent of nonagricultural formal employment and 15.4 percent of total employment in South Africa. Retail/wholesale and construction account for 21.8 and 6.6 percent of nonagricultural formal employment and 24.7 and 7.6 percent of total employment, respectively (Statistics South Africa 2005). Although all three sectors have experienced aggregate growth, employment growth has not kept pace with growth in the labor force. An understanding of the sources of employment growth, wage-setting mechanisms, and the impact of labor regulation is crucial to the execution of vital policies in this arena.

Worker Characteristics

As many as 10 employees per firm were surveyed as part of the data collection exercise. An attempt was made to survey at least one worker from each of the five major occupation categories: managers/proprietors, skilled professionals, technical production workers, unskilled production workers, and nonproduction workers. The manufacturing sector accounts for 82 percent of the workers in the sample; construction and retail/wholesale contribute 8 and 9 percent, respectively. The average worker is 38.5 years old, has 16.2 years of experience, has been with the current firm for 7 years, and has completed just less than 11 years of school. Forty percent of the sampled workers are female. This demographic pattern is uniform across both industry and firm-size categories within industry.

Table 3.1 shows the demographic characteristics of the modal worker in each industry. The modal worker is a technician in the construction sector, an unskilled production worker in manufacturing, and a sales worker in the retail industry. The modal worker in construction and retail/wholesale has about two years of postsecondary education, whereas the modal worker in manufacturing dropped out of school just before acquiring the high school matriculation degree.

The table includes the average demographic characteristics for a sample from the 1994 Labor Force Survey (LFS) conducted by Statistics South Africa. Whereas the average worker in the 1994 LFS is about the same age as the average worker in the employee sample, the former has considerably more experience and less education. Inclusion of primary sectors such as agriculture and mining in the LFS sample most likely accounts for these differences.[1]

Table 3.1 Characteristics of Modal Worker

Sector	*Age*	*Experience*	*Tenure*	*Schooling*
Construction	36.1	14.8	5.2	11.8
Manufacturing	35.9	12.9	5.9	9.8
Retail/wholesale	34.6	12.3	5.2	11.6
1994 labor force survey—private sector	35.7	21.0	—	7.7

Source: Authors.

Remuneration and Determinants of Wages

The nature of the contract between firms and employees determines the extent to which changes in the product market, conditions in the international market, and regulations are likely to affect changes in employment. The type of contract between firms and workers depends on collective bargaining arrangements, monitoring technologies, regulations governing hiring and firing, and prevailing labor market conditions.

Firms were asked to provide total wages for each of the five categories of labor—managers/proprietors, professionals, skilled production workers, unskilled production workers, and nonproduction workers. From these data, average and median monthly wages per worker were computed. Table 3.2 shows median monthly wages for each category and industry.

Median wages in the manufacturing sector range from a low of 2,800 rand per month for unskilled production workers to 20,000 rand per month for managers. With the exception of managers and professionals in the retail/wholesale industry, the median monthly wage for each occupational category is uniform across industry. Managers in the retail/wholesale industry earn 25 and 17 percent less than their counterparts in manufacturing and construction, respectively. Unskilled production workers in all sectors earn a median monthly wage of between 2,600 and 3,000 rand per month. The last column of table 3.2 shows that median wages in manufacturing are higher than median wages in the two services sectors, probably because of the skill composition of labor in each of these sectors; a higher proportion of skilled workers are in the manufacturing sector. This finding is consistent with estimates from the 2003 Statistics South Africa survey of enterprises (Statistics South Africa 2003).

Figure 3.1, which shows average monthly wages for skilled and unskilled workers broken down by firm size class, reveals two striking patterns. First is a large and persistent skill wage premium across industry and size

Table 3.2 Firm-Level Estimates of Median Monthly Salary
(thousands of rand)

Industry	*Managers/ owners*	*Professionals*	*Skilled production workers*	*Unskilled production workers*	*Nonproduction workers*	*Total*
Construction	18.00	15.00	6.00	2.60	4.00	5.20
Manufacturing	20.00	13.00	7.00	2.83	4.00	6.70
Retail/wholesale	15.00	10.00	7.00	3.00	4.00	5.87
Total	**20.00**	**12.76**	**7.00**	**2.83**	**4.00**	**6.38**

Source: Authors.

Figure 3.1 Firm-Level Wages in South Africa, by Industry and Enterprise Size

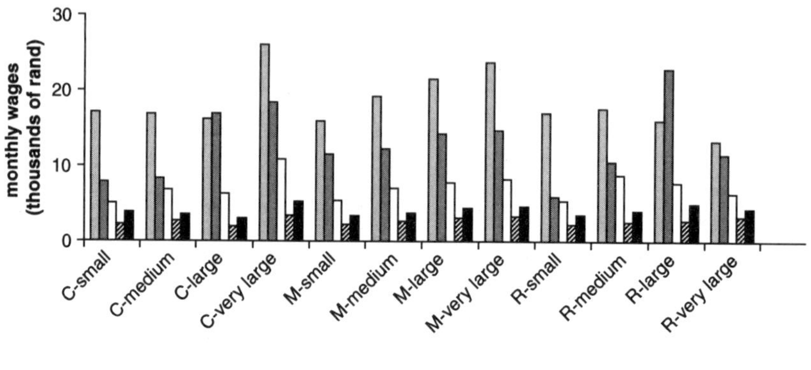

Source: Investment Climate Surveys.
Note: C = construction; M = manufacturing; R = retail.

class. The earnings ratio for managers relative to unskilled production workers in all sectors and size classes ranges from 3 to 5.3 and has a mean of 4.5, which is consistent with recent estimates from LFSs that suggest ratios close to 5 (Mwabu and Shultz 1998). This skill premium is unusually high (see international comparisons below).

Second, in all industries and for all occupations, larger firms pay higher average wages than smaller firms. This association between average wages and firm size is strongest in the manufacturing sector. For skilled workers, the gradient rises from a monthly wage of 5,000 rand in small firms to about 8,200 rand in very large firms. The gradient for managers is even steeper, rising from 16,000 rand in small firms to 24,000 rand in large firms. This wage-firm size association is prevalent, albeit weaker, among unskilled production and nonproduction workers.

These patterns provide prima facie evidence for the wage-determining mechanisms in South Africa's formal labor market. Identifying the predominant wage-setting mechanisms is essential if policy makers are to implement effective labor market policies. The wage-firm size and skill premium patterns observed above suggest three wage-setting mechanisms: (1) collective bargaining, (2) efficiency wages, and (3) fairness norms.

Under the collective bargaining mechanism, workers and firm owners agree to share firm surplus. The respective share that accrues to the bargaining parties is a function of bargaining power. Bargaining power for workers is high when workers are unionized or when individual nonunionized workers possess scarce skills. South Africa has historically had industrial councils and high levels of unionization (Butcher and Rouse 2001; Boccara and Moll 1997). For worker-firm bargaining to be consistent with the firm size-wage patterns observed above, unionization rates must be higher in large firms, and profit levels or union bargaining power must be higher for large firms. Table 3.3 presents some evidence in support of this hypothesis. In all industries, large firms have the highest unionization rates. Furthermore, unionization rates are highest in manufacturing, where 56 percent of the workforce belongs to a union, compared with 28 percent in the retail/wholesale sector.

Value added per worker increases weakly with firm size. Average value added per worker is higher for large and very large firms relative to small and medium-size firms. For these two pieces of evidence to support the collective bargaining mechanism, the bargaining power of unions must be uniform or increase with firm size. Although the evidence appears to support the collective bargaining mechanism, several problems arise. First, although unionization rates increase with firm size, unionization is predominantly concentrated in the unskilled and nonproduction worker categories (see table 3.4, which shows the percentage of workers unionized by industry and occupation[2]).

Second, in the traditional wage bargaining model, collective bargaining employment terms are superior to individually negotiated terms. The wage-firm size pattern should be strongest for skilled and unskilled production workers. Instead, a much stronger pattern for management wages is observed.

Table 3.3 Percentage of Workers Unionized as Reported by Firms

Industry	*Small*	*Medium size*	*Large*	*Very large*	*Total*
Construction	20.5	40.0	34.6	52.5	32.7
Manufacturing	37.2	53.8	64.8	69.8	55.9
Retail/wholesale	16.5	56.6	24.6	27.4	28.0
Total	**31.3**	**52.7**	**59.1**	**65.1**	**50.4**

Source: Authors.

Table 3.4 Percentage of Workers Unionized as Reported by Workers

Industry	*Managers/ professionals*	*Skilled production*	*Unskilled production*	*Nonproduction*	*Total*
Construction	6.9	14.7	27.3	14.6	11.6
Manufacturing	7.0	37.3	45.6	22.0	27.7
Retail/wholesale	1.9	7.7	21.1	8.7	7.5

Source: Authors.

Third, figure 3.1 shows uniform median wages across industry for skilled, unskilled, and nonproduction workers. This finding is inconsistent with the wage distribution predicted by patterns in profitability and unionization across the three industries. Industrial councils probably do not govern this uniformity.

The strong wage-firm size pattern, particularly for management workers, does not support the traditional wage bargaining model, given that less than 10 percent of all managers are unionized. Rather, the evidence is consistent with a hybrid model of individual bargaining for high-skilled workers and collective bargaining for low-skilled workers. Given widespread firm perceptions that high-skilled labor is scarce, bargaining power for managers and professionals is high even though wage bargaining in these two occupations is bilateral.[3]

The second mechanism that is consistent with the wage-firm size patterns outlined above is the efficiency wage model. The crucial feature of this mechanism is the design of incentives when owners cannot monitor employees perfectly. As firms become larger or the nature of the production activity becomes more complex, the cost of monitoring employees rises. To induce worker effort in the presence of weak monitoring, firms must pay higher wages so that the cost of losing a job is significant to the worker's effort-shirking decision. The cost of losing a job depends on the skill-specific unemployment rate. Workers in occupations with a high ratio of job seekers to vacancies face higher unemployment costs. For workers in such occupations, the wage paid need not be very high. However, for workers with low unemployment rates, wage rates should be sufficiently high.

The foregoing discussion has three implications. First, a wage-firm size gradient within industry should be observed as monitoring costs rise with firm size. Second, differences in wages across industry (within firm size) should be observed as production complexity changes. Third, the slope of the wage-firm size gradient should be higher for occupations for which unemployment rates are low. The patterns in figure 3.1 are broadly consistent with the predictions of this model. Steep wage gradients both within and across industry are consistent with variation in the difficulty of monitoring, and wage-firm size gradients are steepest among occupations with the lowest unemployment rates (Statistics South Africa 2005).[4]

These observations can be reconciled by the strength of within-firm wage distribution fairness norms with regard to remuneration of low- and high-skilled workers. These norms could reflect collective beliefs about the marginal contribution of workers from all occupational categories. Alternatively, these norms might be inherited from the apartheid era, during which occupational (and consequently earnings) segregation was strictly enforced.[5] For this mechanism to be consistent with the data, equality norms must be more strongly enforced in small firms, and norms in manufacturing must be less binding than norms in retail and construction. However, in the absence of concrete data on attitudes of firms and workers to wage inequality, this explanation of wage-setting behavior in South African firms remains plausible.

Finally, many researchers have suggested that trade liberalization, skill-biased technical change, and emigration of skilled workers are associated with the persistent and large gap between high- and low-skill wages in South Africa (Fedderke, Shin, and Vaze 2003; Bell and Cattaneo 1997; Nattrass 1998; Bhorat 1999; Birdi, Dunne, and Watson 2001; Brown and others 2002). This possibility can be investigated by examining the evolution of real wages by occupation/skill level using current and starting-level wages from the employee survey.

Figure 3.2 shows annual real wage growth rates for skilled and unskilled workers since 1989. The wage growth series is constructed by calculating the annualized growth in wages for a worker currently employed in the same occupation as his or her starting occupation. Also shown is a time profile (Brown and others 2002) of emigration of skilled workers to New Zealand between 1989 and 1997.

In the period before 1990, wage growth for skilled workers averaged just under 5 percent; in the same period, unskilled workers experienced

Figure 3.2 Wage Growth, 1985–2003

Source: Investment Climate Surveys.

little if any wage growth, which is consistent with increasing prices of skill-intensive goods during the period of import-substitution.

The year 1990 marks a structural break in the wage growth profile of both skilled and unskilled workers. After 1990, wage growth rates rise for both skilled and unskilled workers; in the period between 1991 and 1998, wage growth of skilled workers exceeds that of unskilled workers. This phenomenon coincides with the period of increased outflows of skilled workers. Between 1999 and 2003, unskilled wage growth exceeds that of skilled wage growth, probably due to trade liberalization, which has moved product prices in favor of unskilled-labor–intensive products. These associations are consistent with explanations of the inequality profile in South Africa over this period. The effects of emigration at the onset of majority rule and the effects of trade liberalization favoring unskilled labor widened inequality during the import substitution period (Fedderke, Shin, and Vaze 2003; Edwards and Behar 2006).

To establish which of these mechanisms is most salient, a regression framework that controls for potential explanatory variables is needed. Table 3.5 shows the results of a regression of the log of average monthly wages for each of the job categories on a set of explanatory variables meant to capture the mechanisms and processes outlined above. The regression includes controls for firm size and sector to account for differences in monitoring costs, as well as foreign ownership, export status, age and age squared, and share of workers with 10 or more years of schooling to control for firm quality. Finally, the regression includes the percentage of workers unionized as a measure of differences in bargaining power and total factor productivity to proxy for the size of available rents. The results for each of the job categories are shown in columns 1–4 and the average firm wage is shown in column 5 in table 3.5

Firm size (the omitted category is small firms) explains a significant proportion of variation in average monthly wages for managers, skilled workers, and unskilled production workers. Holding all other factors constant, a manager in a medium-sized firm (50–99 employees) earns about 18 percent more than a manager in a firm with fewer than 50 employees. The wage gap is much larger for very large firms, where managers earn nearly 40 percent more. This wage-firm size profile is also apparent in the determination of unskilled wages; unskilled workers in very large, large, and medium-size firms earn 32, 26, and 14 percent more, respectively, than unskilled workers in a small firm.

The relationship between firm size and average wages is consistent with the efficiency wage theory that predicts higher wages as monitoring

Table 3.5 Determinants of Wages: Firm-Level Estimation

	(1) Managers	(2) Professionals	(3) Skilled	(4) Unskilled	(5) Total
50–99 employees	0.179	−0.011	0.203	0.142	0.162
	(0.062)**	(0.116)	(0.088)*	(0.067)*	(0.103)
100–499 employees	0.253	0.175	0.084	0.263	0.217
	(0.073)**	(0.127)	(0.161)	(0.075)**	(0.120)
More than 500 employees	0.370	0.140	0.279	0.321	0.190
	(0.075)**	(0.159)	(0.118)*	(0.092)**	(0.127)
Firm exports > 10% sales	0.139	0.098	−0.048	0.082	0.225
	(0.055)*	(0.112)	(0.161)	(0.067)	(0.121)
Firm foreign owned	0.040	−0.056	0.081	0.017	0.125
	(0.057)	(0.119)	(0.116)	(0.080)	(0.101)
Firm age	0.055	0.102	0.089	0.045	−0.041
	(0.019)**	(0.050)*	(0.040)*	(0.035)	(0.042)
Firm age squared	−0.001	−0.001	−0.001	−0.001	0.000
	(0.000)**	(0.001)	(0.000)*	(0.000)	(0.000)
% workers 6–9 years	0.002	0.004	0.003	0.001	−0.004
schooling	(0.002)	(0.002)	(0.002)	(0.002)	(0.003)
% workers 10–12 years	0.003	0.003	0.001	0.004	0.002
schooling	(0.001)*	(0.003)	(0.002)	(0.002)**	(0.002)
% workers >12 years	0.004	−0.003	0.015	0.003	0.008
schooling	(0.002)	(0.004)	(0.003)**	(0.003)	(0.003)**
% workers unionized	0.001	0.000	0.003	0.002	−0.001
	(0.001)	(0.002)	(0.001)*	(0.001)	(0.001)
Constant	7.973	6.666	6.162	6.280	9.728
	(0.413)**	(0.981)**	(0.846)**	(0.645)**	(0.893)**
Observations	315	193	309	296	386
R-squared	0.25	0.19	0.20	0.23	0.12
F-test firm size matters	8.34	1.45	2.86	5.50	1.35
Prob>F	0.00	0.23	0.04	0.00	0.26

Source: Authors.
Note: Robust standard errors are in parentheses; * significant at 5 percent; ** significant at 1 percent. Dependent variable is log (average monthly wage in thousands of rand).

costs rise. Holding other factors constant, large and very large firms pay an additional 700 to 900 rand per month for an unskilled worker than small firms. Although unobservable differences in worker quality cannot be ruled out, they are unlikely to account for a 25 to 30 percent difference in the average monthly wage for an unskilled worker.

To test for sensitivity of wages to profitability, total factor productivity is included in corresponding regressions to the specification shown in table 3.5. The results suggest that productivity has a strong effect on wages. The effect is strongest for skilled workers: a 1 percent increase in firm productivity is associated with a 0.7, 0.95, 1.8, and 0.7 percent increase in monthly wages for managers, professionals, skilled workers, and unskilled workers, respectively.

The wages of skilled workers are sensitive to the proportion of workers with more than 12 years of schooling. A percentage point increase in the proportion of workers with more than 12 years of schooling is associated with an increase in the monthly wage of skilled workers of 1.5 percent. The wages of managers and unskilled workers are sensitive to the proportion of workers with 10 to 12 years of schooling. A percentage point increase in the proportion of workers with 10 to 12 years of schooling is associated with an increase in monthly wages of 0.3 percent and 0.4 percent for managers and unskilled workers, respectively. These results suggest important labor externalities in production and underline the importance of increasing the level of skills in the private sector.

No evidence for the profit-sharing mechanism is found. The coefficient on the proportion of unionized workers, although positive in all specifications, is only statistically significant in specification 3. The size of the estimate is also small in economic terms. According to specification 3, a percentage point increase in the proportion of unionized workers is associated with a 0.3 percent increase in average wages. As observed earlier, firm responses to nonunionized workers could diminish the union effect.

Measures of firm quality are also associated with higher wages. Exporting firms pay 14 percent higher wages to managers, all other factors being equal. Similarly, older firms pay higher wages to managers and skilled workers. The association between firm quality and wages can arise, because workers with higher unobservable quality match with better firms. The other reason could be that higher-quality firms are less likely to be liquidity constrained and therefore can pay efficiency wages.

The wage-setting mechanism is further explored using individual-level data from a sample of workers interviewed during the survey (see table 3.6). Sampled workers were asked to report current wages and payment frequency. All reported wages are converted into monthly wages; observations corresponding to the top and bottom 5 percent of the wage distribution, which are likely to reflect erroneous payment frequencies, are dropped.

A major source of estimation bias arises if workers with high (unobservable) quality match with good firms. To determine the extent to

Table 3.6 Median Monthly Wages and Average Schooling, Individual-Level Data

	Construction				*Manufacturing*				*Retail*			
Size class	*10–49*	*50–99*	*100–499*	*>500*	*10–49*	*50–99*	*100–499*	*>500*	*10–49*	*50–99*	*100–499*	*>500*
Managers/professionals												
Monthly wage	13.6	10.8	13	12.4	10.9	10.7	11.5	12.3	10.2	8.2	12.8	9.4
Schooling	11.7	11.9	11.7	11.9	12.1	12.1	12.1	12	12.5	12.9	12.1	12.2
Production and nonproduction workers												
Monthly wage	5	5.4	7.3	6.8	4.2	4.2	4.7	5.5	4.4	4.1	5.1	5.6
Schooling	11.1	10.8	11.2	10.4	10.2	10.7	10.4	10.9	11.1	10.5	11.3	11.4

Source: Authors.

which this worker/firm sorting might be a problem, median monthly wages and average schooling are tabulated by size class, industry, and occupation category. The results strongly suggest the absence of sorting on observable characteristics. Median levels of schooling are generally uniform across size-class categories.[6] As with the firm-level regressions above, the employee wage firm-size gradient is apparent—most strikingly in the manufacturing sector.

The decision to acquire education or further on-the-job training is in part determined by labor market returns to these activities. Individual-level data are used to estimate these labor market returns in a Mincer framework (Mincer 1974). Employer-employee matched data are exploited to control for observable differences in firm quality that might otherwise bias estimates due to sorting.

The results of these estimations are shown in columns 1–7 of table 3.7. Returns to schooling in this sample are very high. Controlling for other factors, an additional year of schooling is associated with an increase in wages of nearly 12 percent in the absence of control for occupational categories. Controlling for occupation considerably reduces the estimates to 6.5–7 percent, which is comparable to recent estimates of returns to education in developed economies on the order of 4 to 7 percent (PURE 2001).

Controlling for other factors, females earn about 14 percent less than males in the absence of control for occupation. Differences in occupational categories chosen by females account for a fraction of this gap; a disproportionate fraction of females work in service and nonproduction occupations. Including occupation controls reduces the wage gap to 10 to 11 percent.

Using the estimates in preferred specification 4, wages rise with experience until 22 years and then drop off.

The effect of being in a union depends on a worker's occupation. First, as observed in table 3.4, union membership is concentrated among low-skilled workers. Not surprisingly, the estimates in specification 1, in which no controls for worker type are included, yield a large and negative estimate of the union effect. Including worker controls in specification 2 reduces the union wage gap to 13 percent. However, interacting union membership with worker type suggests that the negative coefficient arises from the worker categories. Nonproduction workers who are union members earn about 22 percent less than nonunionized nonproduction workers. This result, while perverse, probably reflects a category aggregation problem. Nonproduction workers include sales staff and

Table 3.7 Individual-Level Wage Regressions

	Dependent variable: Log of monthly wages						
	(1)	*(2)*	*(3)*	*(4)*	*(5)*	*(6)*	*(7)*
Schooling	0.116	0.070	0.068	0.066	0.064	0.066	0.066
	(0.004)**	(0.004)**	(0.004)**	(0.004)**	(0.004)**	(0.004)**	(0.004)**
Experience	0.055	0.036	0.035	0.035	0.044	0.052	0.052
	(0.004)**	(0.003)**	(0.003)**	(0.003)**	(0.005)**	(0.006)**	(0.006)**
Experience squared	−0.001	−0.001	−0.001	−0.000	−0.001	−0.001	−0.001
	(0.000)**	(0.000)**	(0.000)**	(0.000)**	(0.000)**	(0.000)**	(0.000)**
Female	−0.135	−0.103	−0.109	−0.114	−0.118	−0.110	−0.084
	(0.020)**	(0.019)**	(0.019)**	(0.019)**	(0.019)**	(0.023)**	(0.023)**
Member of union	−0.299	−0.127	−0.074	−0.111	−0.101	−0.085	−0.100
	(0.021)**	(0.019)**	(0.058)	(0.059)	(0.059)	(0.061)	(0.064)
Worker is full time	0.002	0.001	0.001	0.001	0.001	−0.001	−0.001
	(0.001)**	(0.001)	(0.001)	(0.001)	(0.001)	(0.001)	(0.001)
Worker received training		0.211	0.207	0.184	0.163	0.154	0.156
		(0.017)**	(0.017)**	(0.018)**	(0.019)**	(0.022)**	(0.022)**
Worker is skilled/supervisor		−0.564	−0.535	−0.537	−0.544	−0.602	−0.595
		(0.026)**	(0.031)**	(0.030)**	(0.030)**	(0.036)**	(0.036)**
Worker is unskilled		−1.050	−1.150	−1.148	−1.159	−1.194	−1.198
		(0.027)**	(0.031)**	(0.031)**	(0.031)**	(0.035)**	(0.035)**
Worker service/nonproduction		−0.641	−0.601	−0.593	−0.608	−0.632	−0.639
		(0.026)**	(0.028)**	(0.028)**	(0.028)**	(0.033)**	(0.033)**
Log hours worked			0.084	0.077	0.080	0.022	0.037
			(0.072)	(0.067)	(0.069)	(0.060)	(0.062)

(continued)

Table 3.7 Individual-Level Wage Regressions *(continued)*

	Dependent variable: Log of monthly wages						
	(1)	*(2)*	*(3)*	*(4)*	*(5)*	*(6)*	*(7)*
Union*skilled			–0.133	–0.108	–0.126	–0.105	–0.090
			(0.069)	(0.070)	(0.070)	(0.074)	(0.076)
Union*unskilled			0.148	0.171	0.155	0.134	0.163
			(0.066)*	(0.066)*	(0.067)*	(0.069)	(0.072)*
Union*service			–0.235	–0.228	–0.225	–0.232	–0.214
			(0.068)**	(0.068)**	(0.069)**	(0.074)**	(0.076)**
Firm exports >10% sales					0.061	0.045	0.022
					(0.020)**	(0.025)	(0.026)
Firm foreign owned					0.067	0.030	0.022
					(0.022)**	(0.025)	(0.025)
Firm TFP residuals						0.275	0.297
						(0.083)**	(0.083)**
Industry dummies	Included	Included	Included	Included	Included	Included	Included
Firm size dummies				Included	Included	Included	Included
Other controls					Included	Included	Included
Sector dummies							Included
Constant	–0.208	0.997	0.737	0.754	1.064	1.265	1.208
	(0.097)*	(0.094)**	(0.291)*	(0.275)**	(0.317)**	(0.308)**	(0.316)**
Observations	3683	3547	3523	3473	3465	2419	2419
R-squared	0.33	0.56	0.57	0.58	0.58	0.61	0.62
F-test firm size matters				14.23	9.91	5.02	7.36
prob>F				0.00	0.00	0.00	0.00

Source: Authors.

cleaners. Unionization among the latter is more than three times unionization among sales workers. Taking this reality into account, the estimates also show the traditional positive effect of unions. Unskilled workers in unions earn between 14 to 18 percent more than nonunion members.[7]

Individuals who have received training earn about 16 to 24 percent more than individuals who have not when other factors remain the same. Although this result might reflect the fact that firms select (on unobservable traits) better workers to receive training, the returns are sufficiently large to warrant individuals' financing of their own training.

Tests of the hypothesis that firm size does not matter are all rejected at the usual levels of significance, suggesting that even in the presence of control for observable individual characteristics, an individual in a large firm earns more than an otherwise similar individual in a small firm.

Both firm- and individual-level regressions provide tentative evidence that wage-setting behavior in South Africa is motivated by efficiency wage considerations. To the extent that this is the case, immediately increased employment growth will not necessarily accompany improvements in firm prospects. The role of labor market regulations is crucial in this respect. Emphasis should be placed on firms' capacity to provide the right incentives to work and to monitor workers' effort levels.

Employment Growth

Employment growth is at the heart of the South African government's policy to redress historical inequalities and reduce unemployment. Understanding the sources of employment growth informs the set of policy choices required to achieve this goal. As table 3.8 shows, overall growth between 2001 and 2002 is positive for all three sectors; construction employment growth leads the other two sectors at 13 percent. Job creation in the manufacturing and retail sectors is uniform between 2000 and 2002 at roughly 4.5 percent per year. Growth in temporary labor is strong in the manufacturing sector, averaging nearly 7 percent per year since 2000. Overall, growth in skilled labor matches growth in unskilled labor.

Job creation rates in 2001–02 are only about half as strong as job creation from start up to 2002 (figure 3.3). Whether this finding reflects a current slowdown in the economy or a slowing of growth as firms become older is unclear. Foreign-owned firms experience annual average employment growth of 12 percent per year, compared with

Table 3.8 Employment Growth, 2000–02

	Permanent employment growth 2000/2	*Permanent employment growth 2001/2*	*Temp labor growth 2000/2*	*Temp labor growth 2001/2*
Construction	7.06	13.01	–2.85	–10.59
Manufacturing	4.45	4.36	6.83	11.47
Retail/wholesale	4.75	4.45	3.55	–3.66
Total	**4.79**	**5.44**	**5.48**	**8.02**

Source: Authors.

Figure 3.3 Employment Growth in Manufacturing Sector

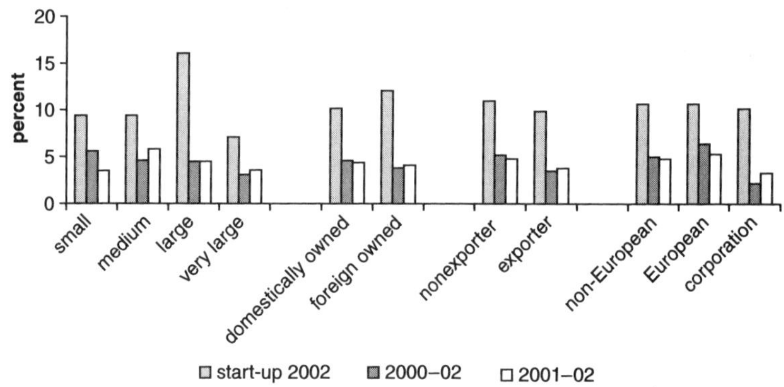

Source: Investment Climate Surveys.

about 10 percent for domestically owned firms. Surprisingly, job creation rates in exporting firms are lower than in nonexporting firms, whether current or long-term growth is examined.

Figure 3.3 shows employment growth for different types of firms in the manufacturing sector. The relationship between job creation and firm size is peculiar. Job creation rates are uniform across small, medium-size, and very large firms; the fastest job creation rates occur in large firms, contrary to recent policy attention to the small and medium-size enterprise (SME) sector (Mazumdar and van Seventer 2004).

Many factors affect the likelihood that a firm will or will not create jobs, including

- idiosyncratic factors, such as local demand shocks that can be proxied by capacity utilization and investment rates;
- measures of firm quality and technology, such as foreign ownership, export status, age, and resource intensity; and

- measures of the business environment, such as the extent to which labor regulation, access and cost of finance, crime, and regulatory policy produce uncertainty.

Many researchers have suggested that the structure of production in South Africa has become more capital intensive in recent years (Fedderke 2005). This explanation is advanced for the persistent and large skill premium and would imply that high investment rates would be accompanied by declining job creation. However, figure 3.4 shows that investment rates in 2001–02 are lower for firms that are *decreasing* employment, suggesting that employment reductions are not driven primarily by substitution away from labor. In support of skill-biased technical change, declines in the number of unskilled workers comprise the major part of permanent jobs shed. Figure 3.4 also shows the complementarity between permanent and temporary labor. Permanent job creation is positively associated with growth in part-time employment. But why are firms that are creating jobs also hiring temporary employment? One reason could be that stringent hiring and firing regulations induce firms to take on temporary labor when they are uncertain of the permanence of positive shocks. Whereas investment rates decline with job shedding, capacity utilization is uniform across firms creating jobs and those shedding jobs.

Firm that shed jobs tend to have an average of 750 permanent workers and 100 temporary workers. Firms that create jobs are smaller, with an average of 250 permanent workers and 40 temporary workers. This finding and the finding that job creation is not necessarily concentrated in

Figure 3.4 Proximate Causes of Employment Growth

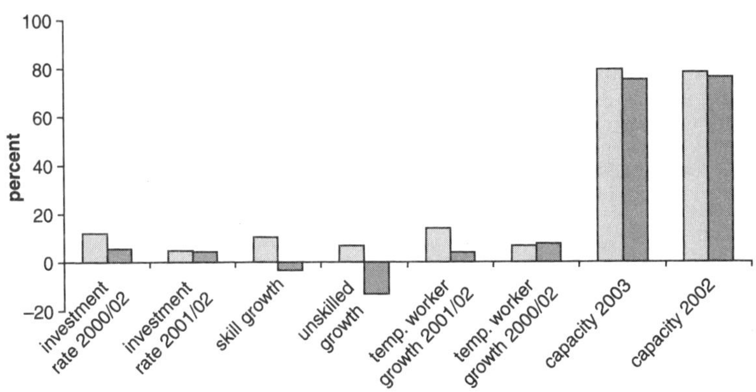

Source: Investment Climate Surveys.

the smallest firms suggest an important caution in implementing SME policies. Such policies should not be restricted to traditional notions of very small firms and should embrace established mid-size firms that have the capacity to use inputs most efficiently.

With respect to the proportion of firms experiencing declines or positive changes in employment, no difference between exporters and non-exporters or between foreign and domestic firms is observed. This finding suggests that between 2000 and 2002, changes in exchange rates and associated export competitiveness were not responsible for employment growth. About 75 percent of firms that shed jobs were established before 1994, compared with about 66 percent of job-creating firms. Evidence that white-owned firms are more likely to experience positive employment growth is weak. Job shedding is concentrated in corporate firms.

To what extent do business environment variables affect the likelihood of employment growth? Firms' investment decisions are made on the basis of expectations about operating constraints. Prominent among these constraints are business environment indicators that underpin future costs of conducting business. Firms that perceive higher costs of doing business are less likely to invest, other factors being constant.

Figure 3.6 shows that 40 percent of firms that shed jobs between 2000 and 2002 report that labor regulations are severe or major constraints, compared with less than 30 percent of firms with positive employment growth. Similarly, a higher proportion of firms shedding jobs report the shortage of skilled labor as a severe or major constraint to operation than firms that created jobs. This finding implies that several

Figure 3.5 Sources of Employment Growth

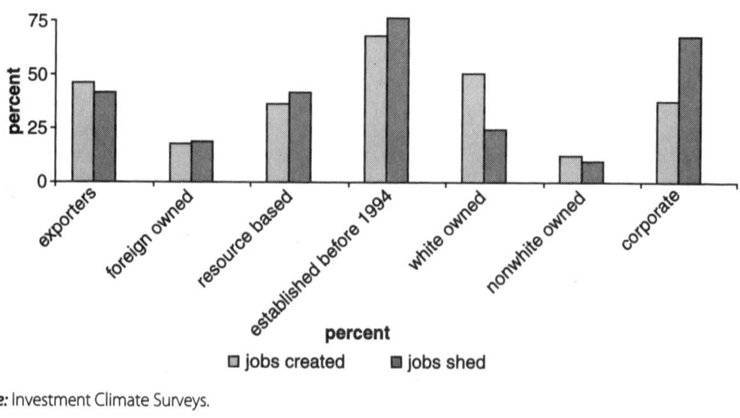

Source: Investment Climate Surveys.

Figure 3.6 Constraints on Employment Growth

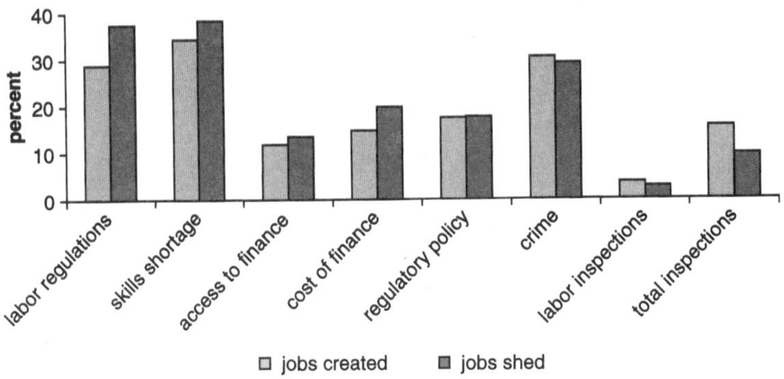

Source: Investment Climate Surveys.

business environment indicators are sufficiently salient to be highlighted by struggling firms.

About 20 percent of firms experiencing negative growth report that cost of finance is prohibitive, compared with about 15 percent of firms with positive growth. Differences across the two employment growth categories in the extent to which crime and policy uncertainty constrain employment growth are not major. Similarly, no evidence that declining firms experienced a higher intensity of labor regulation is found.

Consider wage setting in the manufacturing sectors of a set of comparator countries: Brazil, China, and Poland. Median monthly wages in Brazil and South Africa exhibit strong wage-firm size patterns, particularly in the highly skilled labor categories. Wages in China and Poland are generally uniform across firm size, indicating minimal intraindustry wage differentials. Figure 3.7 shows striking differences in remuneration across countries. The median wage of a manager of a very large firm in China is less than the median wage of an unskilled worker in Brazil and South Africa. This finding highlights an important challenge to the private sector in South Africa—remaining competitive against labor-abundant economies such as China while absorbing the large pool of out-of-work unskilled labor.

Median monthly wages in South Africa are considerably higher than those in most of the comparator countries. The median wages of unskilled workers are a driver for foreign direct investment in textiles and other labor-intensive industries. At US$241 per month, wages for unskilled workers in South Africa are second only to those in Poland, about four times higher than those in China.

Figure 3.7 Cross-Country Comparison of Wages

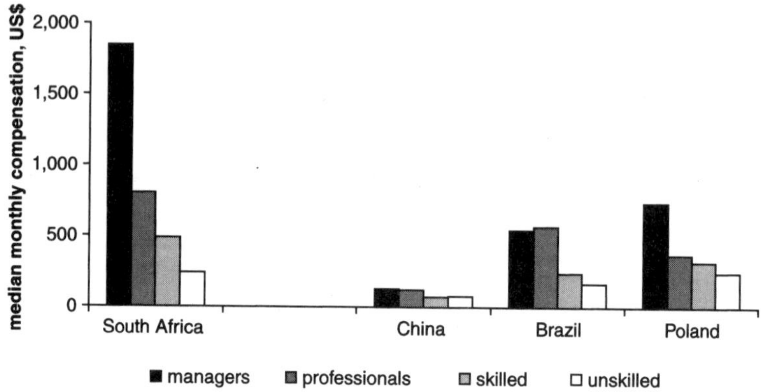

Source: Investment Climate Surveys.

Figure 3.8 Median Time Needed to Fill Vacancies for Skilled and Unskilled Positions

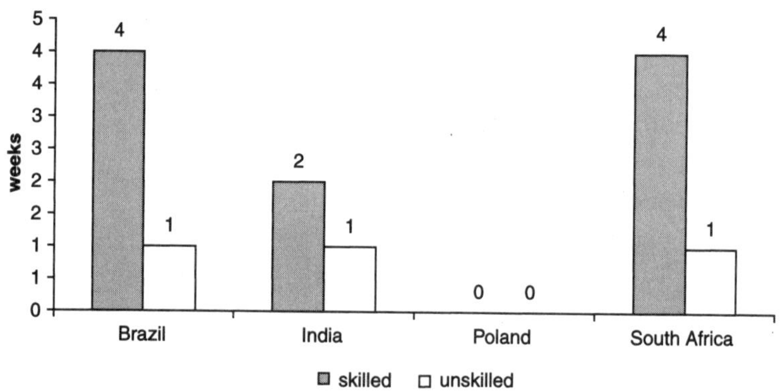

Source: Investment Climate Surveys.

Management in South Africa is highly paid relative to other job categories. Managers in South Africa earn a median monthly wage that is 2.5 and 3 times as large as in Poland and Brazil. South African managers earn nine times as much as unskilled workers, compared with average multiples of 3.2, 3, and 1.7 for Brazil, Poland, and China, respectively.

An important determinant of wages across the different countries is the scarcity of the different categories of labor. Figure 3.8 shows the median number of weeks required to fill a vacancy for skilled and unskilled workers.

Firms in Brazil, India, and South Africa need only a median of one week to fill an unskilled vacancy. To fill a skilled vacancy, firms require a median of four weeks in Brazil and South Africa and two weeks in India. Median vacancy-fill times in Poland for skilled and unskilled labor are less than one week.

Many commentators have suggested that high levels of emigration of skilled workers are creating upward pressure on wages for skilled jobs in South Africa (Brown and others 2003). Assuming that vacancy time is a good indicator of the scarcity of skilled labor, figure 3.8 does not provide strong evidence for this claim. Wages could be determined by future expectations of scarcity, which would be consistent with the link between emigration and wages.

Training

The shortage of skills is one of the leading constraints reported by manufacturing firms in South Africa. Training represents one way to address the scarcity of skilled labor and is crucial to maintaining a competitive labor force, especially in South Africa, where a significant fraction of the population has low levels of schooling. For this group of individuals, on-the-job training represents the single most important channel for augmenting human capital.

Firms in each of the comparator countries were asked to report whether they provide training to workers and to specify the fraction of skilled and unskilled workers offered training. The quality of this training, it should be noted, might differ both within and between countries.

More than 80 percent of unskilled workers receive firm-based training in Poland, 68 percent in Brazil, and 63 percent in China. Less than half

Figure 3.9 Workers Receiving Training, by Country

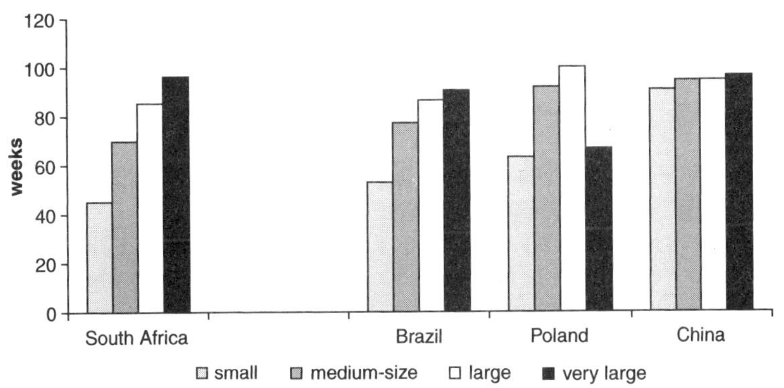

Source: Investment Climate Surveys.

of skilled and unskilled workers in South Africa receive such training—the lowest level provided among the comparator countries (see table 3.9).

However, an examination of the *length* of training offered by firms in each of the comparator countries suggests that South Africa does not lag behind in the amount of training offered. Median training time in South Africa is 14 days, compared with about 3 days in Brazil and 2 days in India.

Sampled workers were asked whether they had received training and how the training was financed. Figure 3.10 reveals a discrepancy in the numbers reported by personnel managers and those reported by individual workers. Just over 80 percent of sampled workers report having received no training. The financing of training is borne by firms across all size categories. Small firms rely on training provided outside the firm, whereas large firms provide some internal training.

The data at hand do not permit an examination of the external sources of training accessible to firms. Given the large fraction of workers who have received no training, training agencies set up by government (SETAs) are crucial in raising human capital levels in South African industry.

Table 3.9 Percentage of Workers Receiving Firm-Based Training

Country	*% of skilled workers*	*% of unskilled workers*
Brazil	77.3	68.3
China	69.1	63.0
Poland	79.9	86.2
South Africa	44.6	45.8

Source: Authors.

Figure 3.10 Share of Workers Receiving Training, by Type and Length of Training

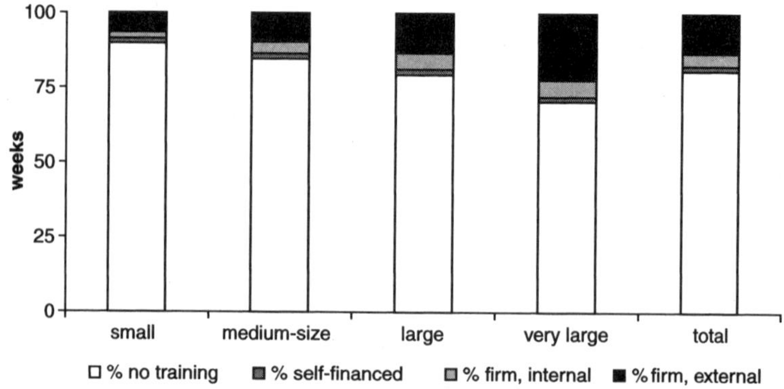

Source: Investment Climate Surveys.

Table 3.10 shows the results of a firm-level Probit estimation of the correlates of the likelihood that a firm offers training to workers. Firm size emerges as a major determinant of firm training. Firms with 50 to 99 workers are 20 percent more likely to provide training than small firms; firms with more than 500 workers are 20 percent more likely to provide training than firms with 50 to 99 workers.[8] Measures of firm quality are strongly associated with the likelihood that a firm provides firm training. A firm that exports is 10 percent more likely to provide training, all other factors remaining the same. Furthermore, foreign-owned

Table 3.10 Determinants of Likelihood That Firms Provide Training

	Dependent variable: Firm offers training indicator			
	(1)	*(2)*	*(3)*	*(4)*
Medium size (50–99 workers)	0.205	0.191	0.196	0.161
	(0.042)**	(0.045)**	(0.046)**	(0.049)**
Large (100–499 workers)	0.311	0.301	0.293	0.287
	(0.039)**	(0.040)**	(0.044)**	(0.045)**
Very large (>500 workers)	0.392	0.390	0.387	0.367
	(0.037)**	(0.037)**	(0.039)**	(0.040)**
Firm exports	0.109	0.057	0.128	0.081
	(0.051)*	(0.058)	(0.053)*	(0.059)
Firm foreign owned	0.171	0.135	0.137	0.109
	(0.050)**	(0.056)*	(0.052)**	(0.059)
Firm age	0.005	0.004	0.003	0.001
	(0.003)	(0.003)	(0.003)	(0.004)
Firm age squared	–0.000	–0.000	0.000	0.000
	(0.000)	(0.000)	(0.000)	(0.000)
Percentage of workers unionized	–0.001	–0.001	–0.002	–0.003
	(0.001)	(0.001)	(0.001)**	(0.001)**
Proportion of temp. workers in workforce	0.074	0.065	0.149	0.110
	(0.043)	(0.039)	(0.098)	(0.100)
Percentage of workers with 6–9 years of schooling		–0.002		–0.003
		(0.001)		(0.001)*
Percentage of workers with 10–12 years of schooling		–0.002		–0.002
		(0.001)		(0.001)
Percentage of workers with > 12 years of schooling		0.001		–0.001
		(0.002)		(0.002)
Sector controls	No	No	Yes	Yes
Observations	733	606	569	483
F-test firm size matters	73.43	62.44	55.46	48.11
prob>F	0.00	0.00	0.00	0.00

Source: Authors.

Notes: Robust standard errors are in parentheses. * significant at 5 percent; ** significant at 1 percent.

Table 3.11 Reasons That Firms Do Not Provide Training

Variable	*% firms reporting reason for no training*
Cannot define/prioritize training needs	10.1
Lack of training institutions for external needs	10.1
Lack of training by chambers of industry, business associations for external training	7.3
Cannot identify competent trainers for internal training	8.7
Cannot afford formal internal or external training	32.2
Lack of government incentives for training	26.9
Workers are uninterested in learning new skills	12.6
Too risky—trained staff may leave	5.6
Too risky—unsure of continuing demand for new skills	7.0
No need—staff can train on the job	84.7
No need—can hire staff from other firms	30.7

Source: Authors.

firms are about 15 percent more likely to provide training than similar nonforeign-owned firms. Surprisingly, a 10 percentage point increase in the proportion of workers who are unionized is associated with a 2 percent reduction in the likelihood that training is provided. Why? Perhaps strong unions constrain firms from providing training to a select group of workers. Finally, a 10 percentage point increase in the proportion of workers with 6 to 9 years of schooling reduces by 3 percent the likelihood that training will be provided.

Table 3.11 suggests that demand, cost, and access are the most important reasons for not providing training. Eighty-five percent of the firms that do not provide training report that training is unnecessary, because workers can learn on the job; 32 percent report that they cannot afford training; 27 percent report that government incentives are insufficient to induce firm-based training; 13 percent report that workers are uninterested in acquiring training; 10 percent report that appropriate training facilities are lacking; and 9 percent report that they cannot identify competent trainers to provide internal training.

Labor Regulation

Surveyed managers were concerned about the impact of labor regulation on their enterprises' operations and growth. Thirty-three percent said that labor regulations were a major or very severe obstacle. Only two other problems—worker skills and macroeconomic instability—were more likely to be viewed as major or very severe obstacles.

Previous research has stressed the potential impact of labor regulations. First, a paper on constraints to growth and employment shows that 10 to 15 percent of a sample of SMEs in South Africa reduced employment as a result of the country's four major labor regulations (Chandra and others 2001b). Firms also reported less hiring, substitution of capital for labor, use of temporary labor, and subcontracting (Chandra and others 2001b). Second, a study on the regulatory environment in South Africa noted that firms take 2.7 months on average to retrench an entry-level employee. They spend R 9,000 to hire and R 2,160–2,900 to fire a least-skilled worker. Partly as a result, 40 percent of firms hired fewer workers, used more machinery, hired temporary staff, or subcontracted (Hudson 2003, 6). Lastly, the 2003 *South Africa Human Development Report* discusses a policy bias during apartheid toward capital intensity. This bias took the form of corporate tax incentives, depreciation allowances, tariff rebates, debt financing, subsidized interest rates, and provision of utilities and infrastructure. Since 1994 policies have continued to promote capital intensity at the expense of employment (UNDP 2003).

Burden of Labor Regulation in the International Context

A comparison of South African regulations with regulations in the middle-income comparator countries and countries of the Organisation for Economic Co-operation and Development (OECD) helps illuminate how burdensome the former are for South African businesses. The Doing Business database, maintained by the World Bank, includes several indexes that measure the rigidity of hiring and firing regulations and the cost of firing (World Bank 2004d).[9] The difficulty of hiring index for South Africa is 56, which is higher than that for all of the comparator countries except Brazil and higher than the average for the OECD economies. Given that higher values indicate more restrictive regulation, hiring regulations would appear to be relatively strict in South Africa.

A similar picture emerges for firing restrictions. The difficulty of firing index for South Africa is 60, higher than that for all the comparator countries except Brazil and higher than the average for the OECD economies. However, on one particular measure, the cost of firing an individual in weeks of wages, South Africa performs better. The cost in South Africa is 38 weeks, lower than the average for the OECD economies and several of the comparator countries.

Overall, South Africa performs worse on most measures relative to the comparator countries and performs considerably worse on the two

Figure 3.11 Cross-Country Comparison of Difficulty and Costs of Hiring and Firing

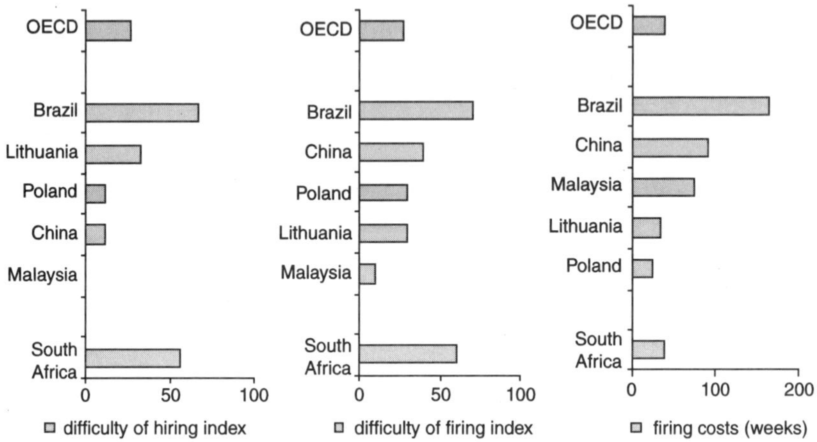

Source: Investment Climate Surveys.

indexes than the OECD countries do. To the extent that South African industry needs to compete with industry in advanced economies, rather than with sometimes poorly performing firms elsewhere in Africa, this assessment is sobering.

South Africa Labor Market Regulations

Four pieces of legislation were passed after apartheid to govern a new labor market in South Africa: the Labor Relations Act (LRA), the Basic Conditions of Employment Act (BCEA), the Equity Employment Act (EEA), and the Skills Development Act (SDA). The more recent Black Economic Empowerment Act (BEE) also affects the country's labor market.

Labor Relations Act of 1995—The LRA of 1995, the first of the four bills passed, remains the most comprehensive piece of labor legislation. It covers employee rights, collective bargaining and union rights, strikes and lockouts, workplace forums, dispute resolution, dismissals, and other general provisions. The LRA stipulates situations in which a dismissal would be classified as unfair. Section 188 states that a dismissal is not automatically unfair but is unfair if the employer fails to prove that the reason for dismissal is a fair reason. Thus, the burden of proof lies with the employer. The Schedule 8 Code of Good Practice for Dismissal lists the three grounds for legitimate termination or fair dismissal: employee conduct, employee capacity, and operational requirement of the business. The employer must prove that the dismissal procedure was fair.

For conduct and capacity reasons, the employer may request a council, accredited agency, or commission to arbitrate allegations concerning the conduct or capacity of an employee. The council, accredited agency, or commission must appoint an arbitrator on receipt of payment by the employer. The LRA does not clarify whether this arbitration is required or optional. If optional, also unknown are how often arbitration occurs, how costly it is (time and money), and how long it takes. Clarification of all of these points would allow researchers to better assess the degree to which the LRA contributes to labor market rigidities associated with employee firing on conduct and capacity grounds.

When the employer dismisses an employee for operational reasons, the employer must consult with any groups required under any collective agreements. If no collective agreement is in place, the employer must consult with affected workplace forums or trade unions. If these do not exist, the employer must consult with the affected employees or their representatives. In these consultations, the groups must attempt to reach consensus on measures to avoid, minimize, change the timing of, and mitigate the adverse effects of dismissals. They must also seek consensus on the methods for selecting employees to be dismissed and for determining severance pay. The employer must issue written notice inviting employees to be dismissed to consult with it and must disclose all relevant information, including reasons for dismissal, alternatives considered and reasons for rejecting each alternative, number of employees affected within the employees' job category, projected time of dismissal, proposed severance, proposed assistance to affected workers, possibility of reemployment, total number of employees within the business, and total number of employees dismissed for operational reasons within the past 12 months. The employer must allow the consulting party to make representations. The employer must consider and respond to each representation; if it disagrees, it must state the reasons for disagreeing. The selection process for dismissed employees must be agreed to or be based on fair and objective criteria. How often the dismissal process for operational reasons takes place, how much it costs, and how long it takes remain unclear.

The Code for Good Practice details procedures recommended before an employee dismissal. They include presenting the allegation to the employee and allowing him or her to prepare a response, disciplinary action, and establishment of a probation period. If a labor court or an arbitrator finds the dismissal to be unfair, it may order reinstatement of, reemployment of, or compensation to the employee. These provisions favor the employee by placing the burden of proof, and much of its cost, on the employer.

Basic Conditions of Employment Act of 1997—The BCEA of 1997 covers working time, leave, remuneration, termination, child and forced labor, sectoral determinations, and monitoring and enforcement. Termination and monitoring are particularly relevant in the present discussion. In the case of a termination, an employee must be notified before dismissal. For an employee who has been with the business four or fewer weeks, one week's notice is required. For an employee with tenure greater than four weeks but less than one year, two weeks is required. For an employee with tenure of one or more years, four weeks notice is required. Severance pay for an employee will equal one week's remuneration for each year of employment.

Chapter 10 of the BCEA focuses on the monitoring and enforcement of labor regulations. The Minister of Labour can appoint any person in public service as a labor inspector. Labor inspectors promote, monitor, and enforce labor regulations. They may enter workplaces at any reasonable time without warrant or notice to question employees and employers and inspect the operations of the business. The act specifies no minimum or maximum number of inspections per business.

Employment Equity Act of 1998—The EEA of 1998 covers the unfair discrimination and affirmative action policies of South Africa, as well as the institutions that govern these policies. Chapter 2 of the act states that a person may not be unfairly discriminated against on the basis of race, gender, pregnancy, marital status, family responsibility, ethnic or social origin, color, sexual orientation, age, disability, religion, HIV status, conscience, belief, political opinion, culture, language, or birth. The burden of proof in discrimination disputes is on the employer.

Chapter 3 of the act focuses on affirmative action. It requires all designated employers to implement affirmative action measures, which are to include identification and elimination of employment barriers that can adversely affect designated groups, as well as measures to advance diversity, to make reasonable accommodations to ensure that designated groups have equal opportunities and are equitably represented, and to ensure representation of suitably qualified people within all occupational categories, as well as to provide for retention and development of said groups. Aside from these measures, employers must consult with employees, conduct analysis to identify barriers, assess diversity levels within occupational categories, and prepare and implement an employment equity plan. When defining the term *suitably qualified,* the act states that a person can have formal qualifications, prior learning, relevant experience, or the capacity to acquire, within a reasonable timeframe, the ability to do the job. It states that employers must assess each of these factors. It emphasizes that employers may not discriminate against a potential employee solely on the grounds of the person's lack of relevant experience.

Section 27 of the chapter on affirmative action focuses on income differentials. Per the BCEA, an employer must submit a statement to the Employment Conditions Commission on the remuneration and benefits received within each occupational category and level. Where disproportionate differentials exist, employers must take measures to reduce these differentials subject to guidance given by the Minister of Labour. Reduction of differentials is likely to lead to some wage inflation.

Skills Development Act of 1998—The SDA of 1998 is geared toward improvement of South African labor force skills through a levy-grant scheme. Difficulty in claiming back the levy has led many small businesses to view the scheme as a tax.

Black Economic Empowerment Act of 2003—The BEE goes beyond the affirmative action of the EEA by setting goals for changing the racial composition of ownership and management structures of existing companies and new enterprises. The BEE allows institutions to pursue the goals in accordance with their BEE plan and the codes of good practice stipulated in the act.

Work Permits

Given the relatively high pay levels for managers and skilled professionals, regulations that affect the ability of firms to employ foreign workers are an important consideration in the present discussion. In general, hiring foreign workers in South Africa is difficult. Work permits will normally not be granted for foreign workers to pursue work for which locals are qualified. However, such workers are welcome if they possess skills that are scarce in South Africa or if they intend to start a business that will result in an infusion of capital from abroad, the manufacture of goods for export, or the employment of South Africans.[10]

The South African Department of Home Affairs examines the following information from employers wishing to obtain a work permit for a foreign national:

- date on which the position became available;
- whether the vacancies were advertised and, if so, in which national papers or other suitable media and the number of insertions (Internet advertising is not acceptable);
- reasons that applicants from the South African labor market who may have responded to the advertisements could not be appointed;
- whether the Department of Labor, private employment bureaus, or relevant trade unions were approached with regard to filling the position;
- whether a local unit can be trained to fill the position, even if a foreign specialist must undertake the task of training for a limited time;
- whether the applicant appointed or to be appointed possesses any exceptional qualifications, training, and experience not obtainable in South Africa; and,
- in the case of senior positions, whether the proper filling of the vacancy or position by the promotion of existing personnel has received due consideration.

The department further stipulates that the applicant must possess a firm offer of temporary employment of a clearly defined maximum duration and that the applicant's proposed position is commensurate with the applicant's qualifications. Professionally qualified persons must register with the appropriate South African bodies. Finally, the applicant must pay a tariff equal to R1 520 ($169 / €152).

Conclusions

Average wages in the manufacturing sector are higher than in the construction and retail sectors, largely due to the composition of skilled labor. Average wages within occupation are uniform across sectors.

Median wages in South Africa are high. The unskilled worker earns US$246 per month, compared with about US$76 per month in China. To remain competitive, South African firms must become considerably more efficient.

Firm size and productivity are significantly associated with wages for management and unskilled workers. These findings are broadly consistent with payment of high wages when effort is difficult to observe and with relatively great bargaining power for managers with respect to productivity gains.

Returns to schooling are high. An extra year of schooling is associated with a 7 percent rise in monthly earnings. The gender gap in earnings is substantial; women earn about 11 percent less than men, all other factors being equal.

Returns to training are high. A worker who has received some training earns about 20 percent more than a worker who has received no training. Although this result is likely to be confounded by unobserved worker ability, it suggests positive returns to training.

Training in South African firms remains lower than the levels required to bolster the human capital of a generation of workers who received insufficient schooling. In addition, high wage levels in South Africa mean that firms must provide rigorous and continuous training to secure and maintain a competitive advantage. SETAs must dramatically improve their performance if they are to meet the training needs of industry.

Notes

1. Although the 1994 sample includes workers in the agricultural, mining, and informal sectors, the sample of workers used here may not be representative of the labor force in manufacturing, trade, and construction because of an unrepresentative sample of workers in the sampled firms or the employment of nontypical workers by firms in this survey.
2. The numbers used to construct this table come from the employee survey. The differences in the unionization rates arise from the fact the data in table 3.3 are derived from the personnel manager at the firm level, whereas the data in table 3.4 are derived from interviews of sampled workers. Sampling and reporting biases could generate the discrepancy observed.
3. Managers and professionals might be paid higher wages to stay out of unions (Pencavel 1995; Lewis 1963).
4. In March 2005 the unemployment rate of white males was 4.4 percent, compared with 26.7 percent for black males. These numbers are indicative of the unemployment rates for skilled and unskilled occupations (Statistics South Africa 2005). More recent research suggests that nearly 80 percent of all firms find it hard or very hard to find managers or professional workers. Only 5 percent of firms surveyed found it hard to find laborers (Bhorat and Lundall 2004).
5. The debate on the extent to which premarket and labor market discrimination has diminished since the onset of majority rule is quite active. Moll (1991)

finds evidence of a reduction in earnings and participation discrimination, whereas Rospabe (1999) presents evidence suggesting a slight increase in unexplained differences in participation and wage earnings.

6. Unobservable differences in schooling quality could remain. However, the data at hand cannot resolve this question.
7. This estimate is at the lower end of estimates by Mwabu and Shultz (1998) but is closer to estimates by Butcher and Rouse (2001).
8. A test of a null hypothesis that firm size does not matter is rejected at the 1 percent level.
9. Note that calculation errors in an earlier version of the World Bank's Doing Business database and a change in methodology resulted in misclassification of South Africa in early versions of the database. These errors have been corrected in the more recent Doing Business reports.
10. See South African Department of Home Affairs, available at http://www.homeaffairs.gov.za/service_detail.asp?id=113.

CHAPTER 4

Access to and Cost of Finance

Enterprise managers often view access to finance and the cost of financing as serious obstacles to their enterprises' operations and growth. In 17 of 49 low- and middle-income countries, over 40 percent of enterprises reported that finance was a major or very severe problem (World Bank 2004b). In most Sub-Saharan African countries, firms rate access and cost of finance among their top five investment-climate–related problems.[1]

Finance as an Obstacle to Enterprise Operations and Growth

In contrast to firms in other countries, firms in South Africa rated neither access to finance nor cost of financing as serious obstacles to enterprise operations and growth. Fewer than 20 percent of enterprises rated either as a major or very severe obstacle. Firms rated access to finance 8th and cost of financing 11th among the 18 constraints queried in the survey. By comparison, over 50 percent of enterprises in the middle-income comparator countries of Brazil and Poland rated cost of financing as a major obstacle, and over one-third rated access to finance as a major obstacle (see figure 4.1). In Kenya and Senegal, over 40 percent of firms rated access to finance and over 60 percent rated cost of financing a serious obstacle. Even in China, the comparator country closest to South Africa

Figure 4.1 Cross-Country Comparison of Firms, by Perceptions of Access to and Cost of Financing and by Inflation and Loan Interest Rate

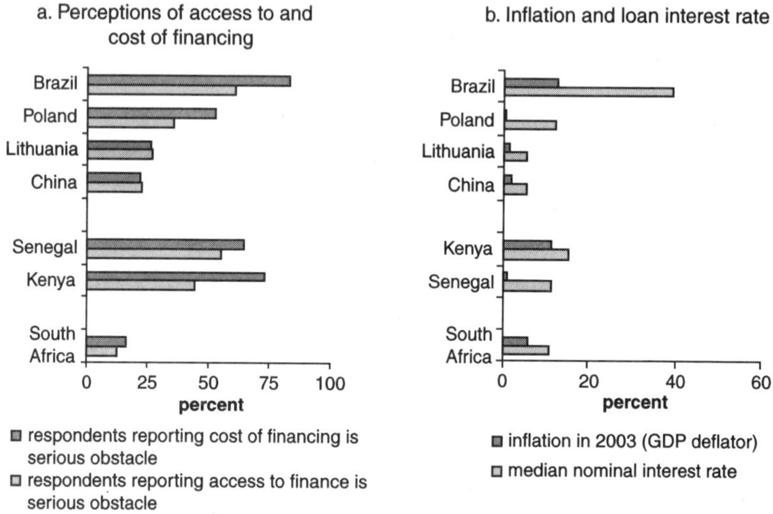

Source: Investment Climate Surveys.

in this respect, about 20 percent of enterprises rated access and cost of financing as major constraints.

Are objective data from the Investment Climate Survey (ICS) consistent with this finding? In some respects, South Africa performs well on objective measures of the cost of finance (figure 4.1). The median nominal interest rate on enterprises' most recent loan was 11 percent—lower than in Poland (12 percent), Senegal (12 percent), Kenya (15 percent), and Brazil (40 percent). Although nominal interest rates were lower in China and Lithuania (about 5.5 percent in both cases), inflation was also lower in these countries. In 2002 and 2003, inflation was 0 and 1 percent, respectively, in Lithuania and –1 percent and 2 percent, respectively, in China. By comparison, inflation in South Africa was 10 percent in 2002 and 6 percent in 2003.[2] In summary, real interest rates appear to be relatively low in South Africa compared with those in other middle-income countries and other countries in Sub-Saharan Africa. This finding is consistent with the perceptions-based data that suggest that most enterprises in South Africa do not view the cost of financing as a serious obstacle.

The next question is whether objective data on access to finance support the view that access is also relatively good in South Africa. Although South Africa's performance appears similar to that of other

Figure 4.2 Cross-Country Comparison of Access to Finance

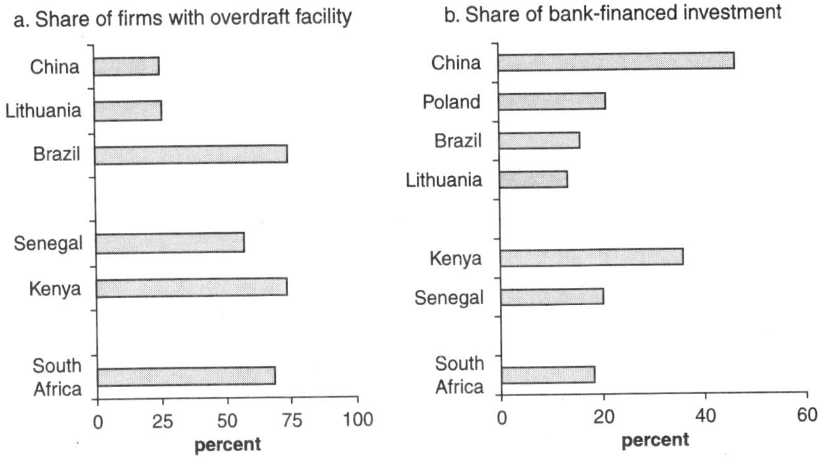

Source: Investment Climate Surveys.

middle-income countries, arguing that South Africa outperforms them on this dimension is hard.

Figure 4.2 shows the percent of firms with overdraft facilities and the percent of new investment that firms finance with funds from local and foreign commercial banks. In general, South Africa performs relatively well, although it does not outperform other countries. About 70 percent of South African firms have overdraft facilities, higher than firms in China (25 percent), Lithuania (26 percent), or Senegal (58 percent) but lower than firms in Brazil or Kenya (both about 74 percent).

South African firms finance about 17 percent of new investment with funds from local and foreign commercial banks. This percent is higher than in Lithuania (12 percent) and Brazil (14 percent) and lower than in Senegal (18 percent), Poland (19 percent), Kenya (32 percent), and China (42 percent). About 36 percent of firms in South Africa had a bank loan, compared with about 39 percent of firms in Kenya, 40 percent in Senegal, and 58 percent in China. In Hangzhou, one of the fastest-growing Chinese cities, nearly 70 percent of firms reported having bank loans. Although South African firms do not appear to be facing a serious financing crunch, they are not as awash with credit as firms in some of the comparator countries.

Another important source of financing, especially for working capital, is trade credit. South African firms rely on trade credit to finance nearly 12 percent of their working capital needs (see figure 4.3). This percent

Figure 4.3 Cross-Country Comparison of Trade Credit

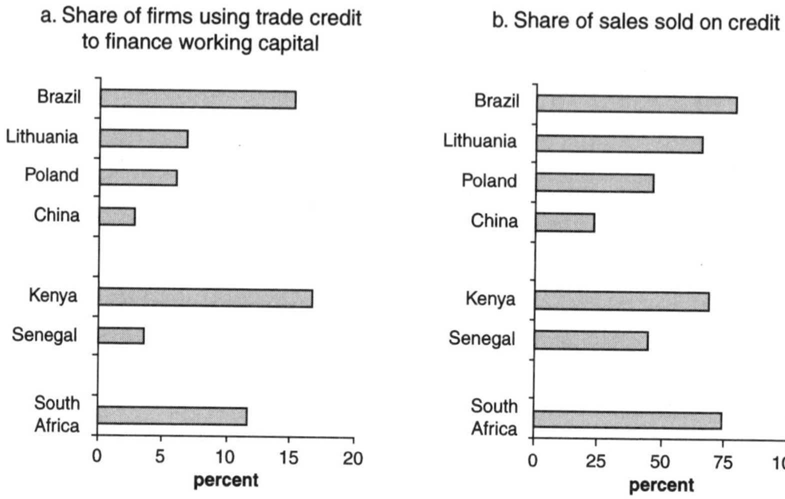

Source: Investment Climate Surveys.

is higher than in any of the comparator countries except Brazil and Kenya. South African firms are also more likely to sell goods on credit than firms in any of the comparator countries except Brazil. This reliance on trade credit and willingness to extend credit to other firms suggests that South African firms are able to enter arms-length deals with other firms and that they believe that they can rely on formal and informal enforcement mechanisms to ensure payment. This finding is consistent with evidence that South African firms trust the court system to uphold their property rights and enforce contracts.

Firms with loans were not particularly concerned about financing. Only 17 percent of these firms rated access to finance and only 22 percent rated cost of finance as a serious obstacle. But many firms without loans were also unconcerned. About 25 percent of South African firms reported that they had never applied for a loan (figure 4.4). These firms were even less likely than firms with loans to rate access or cost of financing as a serious obstacle. Only 6 percent rated access as a serious obstacle, and only 9 percent rated cost as one. When asked why they had not applied for a loan, most of these firms reported that they did not need a loan (72 percent), that they received financing from their parent company (10 percent), or that they did not want to incur debt (10 percent). These findings suggest that many of the firms that have never applied for a loan are relatively credit unconstrained.

Figure 4.4 Loan Status and Reasons for Not Having Loans

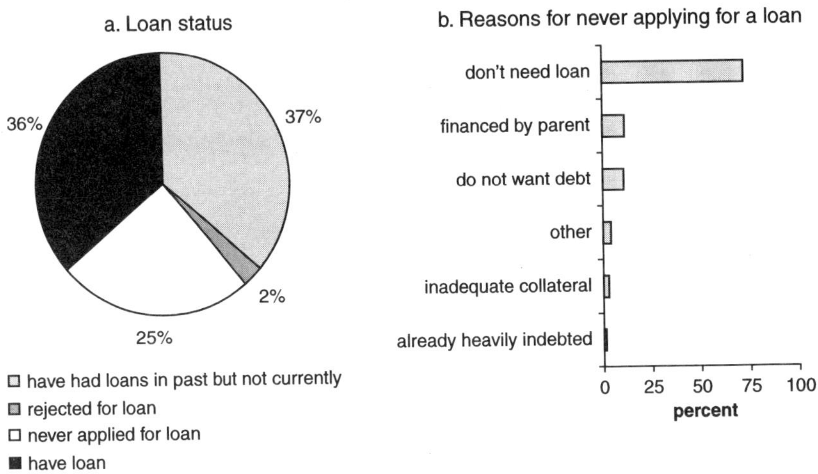

Source: Investment Climate Surveys.
Notes: In figure a, firms are classified as rejected if (1) they do not currently have a loan, and (2) they have been rejected for a loan at some point. Firms that have been rejected but currently have a loan are classified as having a loan. The "rejected" category potentially includes firms that currently have no loan but that had one in the past and were rejected before their previous loan. In figure b, "financed by parent" means that the firm reports receipt of financing by parent company or holding company. Numbers do not add to 100 percent because multiple answers were possible.

About 6 percent of firms reported that they had had a loan application rejected, but many of these firms also reported having loans. About 2 percent of firms reported that they currently had no loan and that they had been rejected for a loan. The latter firms were far more likely to report access to finance and the cost of finance as problems—35 percent reported that access was a serious obstacle, and 41 percent reported that the cost of finance was a serious obstacle.[3]

The remaining 37 percent of firms had had loans in the past but not currently. These firms were not especially likely to rate access to finance or cost of financing as serious obstacles. About 13 percent rated access as a serious obstacle, and 16 percent rated cost as a serious obstacle.

In summary, although South African firms do not appear to use bank financing as much as firms in some other countries (for example, China)—and remain heavily dependent on retained earnings for both investment and working capital (66 percent of working capital and 58 percent of investment)—most do not view access or the cost of financing as a serious obstacle. The low use of bank financing appears to be due to low demand. Most firms that had never applied for a loan reported that they neither wanted nor needed one, and few firms had been rejected for a loan.

Perceptions about Access to Finance by Firm Type

Access to and cost of financing varies across firms. For example, foreign-owned firms in developing countries are often less likely to obtain financing from domestic sources than domestically owned firms. Instead, foreign-owned firms rely on their parent company for financing. Figure 4.5 shows the percent of firms in different categories that rated access and cost of financing as major or very severe obstacles to their operations and growth.

Several interesting patterns emerge from these data. First, small and medium-size firms are more likely to rate access to finance as a serious constraint than larger firms, but no similar pattern for cost of financing was found; very large firms were as likely to complain about the cost as firms in other size categories. Second, foreign-owned firms were far less likely to complain about both the cost of financing and access to finance than domestically owned firms. Exporters were also less likely to view access and cost as serious obstacles. Audited firms were far less likely to report that access was a serious problem but were not more likely to complain about the cost of finance. Older firms—especially those founded before 1994—were less concerned about access than younger firms; no pattern emerged with respect to cost of financing.

Corporate-owned firms were far less concerned about both access and cost than firms owned by individuals and families. One plausible explanation is that corporate-owned firms rely heavily on their parent companies or holding companies for financing.

Figure 4.5 Share of Firms Rating Access to and Cost of Finance as a Major Obstacle, by Size, Ownership, Presence of Audited Accounts, and Age

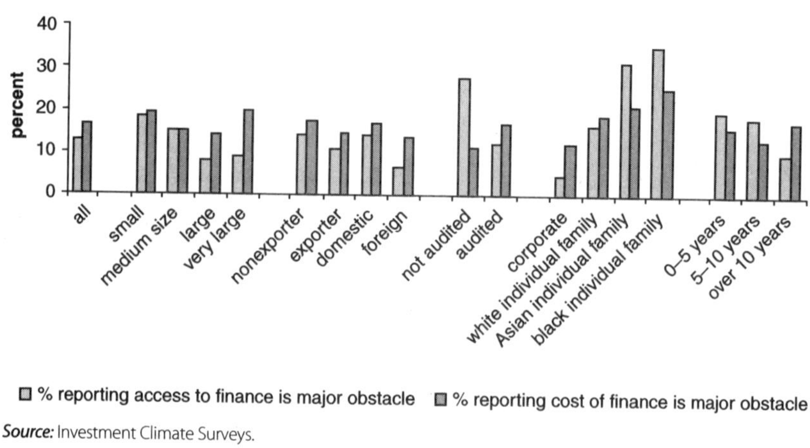

Source: Investment Climate Surveys.

In general, white-owned firms were less likely than black- or Asian-owned firms to rate access and cost as serious concerns.[4] Do the facts that black- and Asian-owned firms tend to be smaller (on average, 110 and 118 employees, respectively) than white-owned firms (128 employees) and to be younger (on average, 19 and 15 years, respectively) than white-owned firms (23 years) explain the difference in perception? To test this hypothesis, multivariate regressions of perceptions about access to finance were run on dummy variables indicating ownership and control variables. After controlling for size, export status, foreign ownership, presence of audited accounts, managers' years of education, and the age of the firm, the difference remained statistically significant for both black- and Asian-owned firms in the regression for access to finance. In the regression for cost of financing, the coefficients remain positive, indicating that black- and Asian-owned firms believe that the cost of financing is a greater obstacle than white-owned firms, but are statistically insignificant. Although the coefficient is statistically insignificant, the small number of black- and Asian-owned firms makes statistically significant results difficult to find (table 4.1).

Although the results of the multivariate regressions are consistent with the idea that black- and Asian-owned firms suffer from discrimination, other explanations are also plausible. These include the omission of unmeasured differences between different types of firms and owners, such as the availability of collateral or the education or business experience of the management team. Moreover, because Africans were actively discriminated against under the previous regime, the analysis' inclusion of some objective indicators such as years of education might not provide an adequate control if quality of education differed by race.[5]

Another possible reason for the differences in the perceptions of black- and Asian-owned firms on the one hand, and white-owned firms on the other, is that these differences might not accurately mirror objective indicators. Perceptions tend to change slowly over time, whereas the underlying objective indicators might change more quickly. To investigate the validity of this explanation, the analysis must be extended to several objective indicators of financial sector performance.

Objective Indicators on Access to and the Cost of Finance

Whether or not a firm views access to and cost of financing as serious obstacles will depend in part on how good the firm's access is (that is, whether it can get a loan). But other factors will also affect the perception. For example, firms owned by larger holding companies might be less concerned about access to finance, because they can get better terms on

Table 4.1 Impact of Ownership on Perceptions about Access to Finance

	Ordered probit			
	Access to finance		*Cost of financing*	
	(high values mean greater obstacle)			
Observations	*586*	*586*	*586*	*586*
Firm characteristics				
Age of establishment	−0.1416**	−0.1362**	−0.0206	−0.0178
(natural log)	(2.51)	(2.44)	(0.42)	(0.36)
Number of workers	−0.0016	−0.0011	0.0532	0.0534
(natural log)	(0.04)	(0.03)	(1.32)	(1.33)
Company has audited accounts	0.0535	0.0465	0.0942	0.0936
(dummy)	(0.16)	(0.14)	(0.35)	(0.35)
Manager				
Manager has university education	−0.1714	−0.1713	−0.3208**	−0.3203**
(dummy)	(1.28)	(1.29)	(2.54)	(2.54)
Globalization				
Any foreign ownership	−0.2071	−0.2005	−0.0881	−0.0859
(dummy)	(1.40)	(1.36)	(0.69)	(0.67)
Exporter	0.0489	0.0504	0.0308	0.0321
(dummy)	(0.45)	(0.46)	(0.31)	(0.32)
Ownership				
Corporation	−0.4381***	−0.4422***	−0.2881**	−0.2898**
(dummy)	(3.53)	(3.57)	(2.52)	(2.54)
Non-European individual/family		0.4704***		0.2296
(dummy)		(3.01)		(1.52)
African individual/family	0.6926***		0.3306	
(dummy)	(2.59)		(1.15)	
Asian individual/family	0.3423		0.1508	
(dummy)	(1.60)		(0.76)	
Colored individual/family	0.5185***		0.3232	
(dummy)	(2.92)		(1.45)	
Pseudo R-squared	0.05	0.05	0.02	0.02

Source: Authors.

loans or because they have less need for outside financing. If they can rely on their parent company for investment when they need financing, they might perceive access to be a lesser concern even if they are no more likely to get a bank loan than a similar firm owned by a family or individual. Similarly, they might be less concerned about the cost of financing (that is, interest rates) if they have access to cheap financing from their parent company.

On some measures, little variation across firm types is observed. For example, the median firm in all categories reported that collateral equal to 100 percent of the loan value was required to get a loan. In addition, the median firm in all categories other than foreign-owned firms reported loan lengths equal to five years. Foreign-owned firms reported a median length of 4.5 years. On other measures, variation across firm types is observed.

Age and Firm Size

Although younger firms were more likely to view access to finance as a constraint, they were also more likely than older firms to have bank loans (46 percent of firms younger than 5 years old, compared with 37 percent of firms older than 10 years) and to finance a greater amount of working capital through bank financing (table 4.2). These numbers probably reflect the fact that younger firms often are less able to finance investment and working capital through retained earnings and that they often have greater investment needs in the short term. Consistent with these likelihoods, younger firms were over twice as likely to have been rejected for loans (11 percent of firms less than 5 years old compared to 5 percent of firms over 10 years old), and the median firm under five years old paid fractionally higher interest rates than older firms (11 percent compared with 10 percent).

Compared with smaller and larger firms, medium-sized firms were less likely to have loans and overdrafts. In addition, they financed less of their working capital through banks (table 4.2). This pattern is different from that observed in most countries, where smaller firms are less likely than larger firms to have bank financing. For example, in Senegal only about 40 percent of small firms had a bank loan, compared with nearly two-thirds of large firms (figure 4.6). Similarly, in China about one-third of small firms had a bank loan, compared with nearly three-quarters of very large firms.

The reason is not that larger firms have lower demand for bank financing. Compared with small firms, very large firms were almost as likely to report being rejected for a loan and were nearly as likely to have applied for a loan. The median very large firm reported lower interest rates than smaller firms—but only slightly lower.

Internationalization

Foreign-owned firms were less likely to have loans or overdraft facilities (34 and 55 percent, respectively) than were domestically owned firms (38 and 70 percent, respectively) (see table 4.2). In addition, they financed less of their working capital with bank financing (14 percent compared with 17 percent for domestically owned firms). The main reason may be that foreign-owned firms have lower demand for bank financing. They were less likely to have ever applied for a loan (58 percent compared with 78 percent for domestically owned firms); none had been

Table 4.2 Financing by Type of Firm

	Percent ever applied for for loan	*Percent with loan*	*Percent with overdraft*	*Percent ever rejected for loan*	*Median interest rate (%)*	*Percent of working capital financed through banks*
All	**75**	**38**	**68**	**6**	**11**	**16.5**
Firm Size						
Small	79	39	73	7	11	17.2
Medium size	73	31	66	9	11	15.2
Large	75	40	64	3	11	16.8
Very large	74	39	75	6	10	16.5
Internationalization						
Nonexporter	76	38	68	7	11	17.3
Exporter	73	37	67	4	10	14.8
Domestic	78	38	70	7	11	16.9
Foreign	58	34	55	0	10	14.3
Accounting						
No audited accounts	56	28	56	11	11	14.7
Audited accounts	76	38	69	6	11	16.7
Ownership						
Corporate	65	33	58	2	10	11.9
Caucasian	84	42	77	9	11	20.3
Asian	79	37	66	14	10.5	20.4
African	70	40	75	10	11.5	12.3
Age						
Less than 5 years	71	46	60	11	11	21.1
5–10 years	69	34	69	5	10.0	14.8
Over 10 years	78	37	70	5	10.5	15.9
Province						
Gauteng	78	35	65	6	10.5	14.0
KwaZulu-Natal	71	38	68	13	11.5	22.1
Western Cape	76	45	77	4	11.0	22.1
Eastern Cape	53	33	72	8	10.8	12.3

Source: Authors.

rejected for a loan. Furthermore, the median foreign-owned firm paid lower interest rates than the median domestically owned firm (10 percent compared with 11 percent).

The difference between exporters and nonexporters was more modest than the difference between foreign- and domestically owned firms. Although firms involved in exporting had fewer loans or overdraft facilities than nonexporters, the difference was not large. They were also less

Figure 4.6 Cross-Country Comparison of Access, by Firm Size

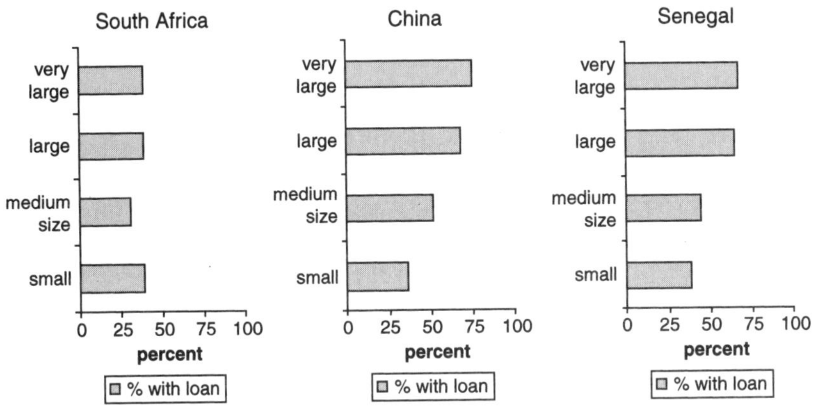

Source: Investment Climate Surveys.

likely to finance their working capital needs through the banking sectors. In this case, the difference is more noticeable; exporters on average finance 15 percent of working capital needs through the banking system, whereas nonexporters finance about 17 percent. Exporters were also less likely to use trade credit. Similar patterns hold for new investment. As a result, exporters rely more heavily on retained earnings to finance both working capital and new investment (69 and 64 percent, respectively) than nonexporters (64 and 55 percent, respectively).

Accounting

Firms without audited accounts were far less likely than firms with audited accounts to have loans and overdraft facilities and were far more likely to have been rejected for a loan—11 percent compared with 6 percent (table 4.2). Ninety-seven percent of firms had audited accounts, which is high compared with firms in other middle-income countries. In comparison, only 80 percent of Brazilian firms and 40 percent of Polish firms had audited accounts. Most of the firms without audited accounts (9 of 18) were small.

Ownership

Compared with firms owned by individuals or families, firms owned by other corporations were far less likely to have loans or overdrafts facilities, and they financed less new investment and working capital through bank finance (table 4.2). They were also far less likely to have ever applied for a loan. Only 65 percent of corporate-owned firms had ever applied for a loan, compared with 83 percent of firms owned by individuals or families.

Corporate-owned firms' apparent lack of reliance on bank financing does not appear to owe to the firms' inability to obtain loans. Only 2 percent of corporate-owned firms reported ever being rejected for a loan, and most firms that had not applied for a loan reported that they did not need one, because they were financed by their parent company or because they did not want to incur debt. Only 2 of 92 corporate-owned firms that had not applied for a loan said that they had inadequate collateral; 2 reported that they were already heavily indebted.

Consistent with the perceptions-based data, black- and Asian-owned firms generally appeared to be less likely to have access to bank financing (table 4.2). The differences in the objective indicators, however, were generally modest. About 40 percent of black-owned firms and 37 percent of Asian-owned firms had a bank loan. In comparison, 42 percent of white-owned firms had a loan. Asian- and black-owned firms were also less likely to have an overdraft facility and were more likely to report that they had been rejected for a loan. Black-owned firms, but not Asian-owned firms, financed less working capital and less investment through banks than white-owned firms. They also relied less than white-owned firms on trade finance to finance working capital and less on leasing to finance new investment (figure 4.7).[6] As a result, they tend to rely more heavily on retained earnings for both new investment and working capital.

Figure 4.7 Working Capital and New Investment

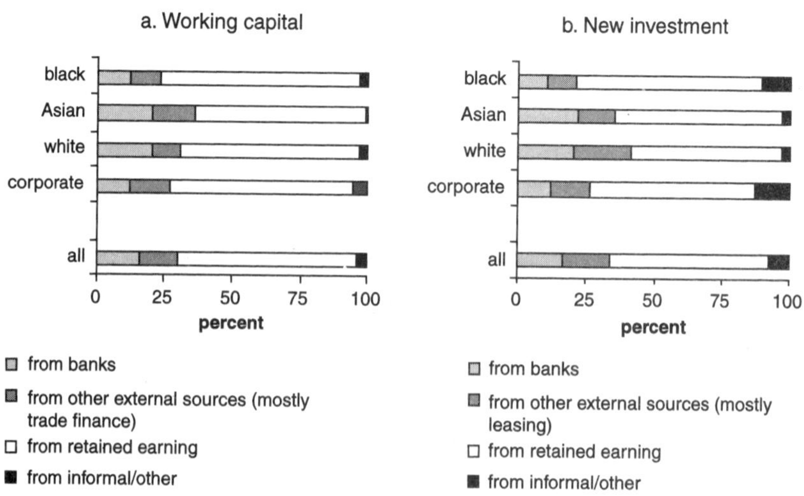

Source: Investment Climate Surveys.

The median black-owned firm also reported paying a higher interest rate (11.5 percent) than the median white-owned firm (11 percent). In contrast, the median Asian-owned firm reported paying a slightly lower interest rate than the median white-owned firm.

Although the objective data are consistent with the perception-based data, the results above must be treated with caution. First, the differences in the objective data are not statistically significantly different from zero at conventional significance levels after controlling for other factors that might affect access to finance. That is, the possibility that the differences are due to random variation cannot be ruled out. Second, as noted above, the differences could be due to unobserved differences among firms (for example, quality of managers or workers' education) for which the empirical analysis has no controls.

Notes

1. For example, cost of and access to financing ranked 1st and 4th in Uganda (World Bank 2004e), 2nd and 11th in Kenya (World Bank 2004c), and 3rd and 6th in Tanzania (World Bank 2004a).
2. Inflation is the change in the implicit GDP price deflator for the relevant years.
3. Firms with loans but that had been rejected for at least one loan were also more likely to report that access and cost were serious obstacles.
4. Because so few firms in the survey are owned by individuals of color, these firms are omitted from this section.
5. See, for example, Fedderke, de Kadt, and Luiz (2000), Case and Deaton (1999), and Selod and Zenou (2003) for discussions of this issue. Selod and Zenou (2003) note, for example, that per capita spending was four times higher for white children than for black children and that the student/teacher ratio was twice as high.
6. Lease financing accounts for nearly all the "other external sources" category for new investment, whereas trade credit accounts for nearly all the same category for working capital.

CHAPTER 5

Other Aspects of the Investment Climate

The Investment Climate Survey (ICS) asks firms to report how serious an obstacle various areas of the investment climate are to enterprise operations and growth. Perception-based measures provide a good starting place for an analysis of the investment climate, because enterprise managers likely have a reasonable grasp of the immediate problems facing their business. But such measures suffer from several drawbacks:

- Firms' experiences and expectations differ significantly among countries. Comparing performance across countries is far easier using objective measures of the investment climate.
- Quantifying and aggregating perception-based data across firms are difficult. Consequently, assessing exactly what would need to be done to reduce a given constraint is difficult.
- Although managers may be aware of a problem, they may not be aware of the underlying causes. For example, a bank loan might be difficult to obtain because of lack of competition in the banking sector, government debt issues crowding out private investment, or problems with land registration that make land difficult to use as collateral.
- Enterprise managers might perceive obstacles differently than potential entrepreneurs. For example, managers who have already completed

registration procedures might not be concerned about entry costs, even if they remain high. Similarly, if transportation costs are especially high in some areas, firms might be located close to transportation facilities. Because only existing enterprises are asked about obstacles, the ICS might miss some issues.

These concerns mean that quantitative data from the ICS and other sources must supplement perception-based data. The additional data allow exploration of questions in greater detail as well as comparison of South Africa's performance with other countries' performance.

Perceptions about Investment Climate Problems

In the ICS, managers were asked whether 18 areas of the investment climate were a problem for their enterprise's operations and growth. They responded using a five-point scale, ranging from "no problem" to a "very severe problem." For each area, the percent of firms that rated it as a "major" or "very severe" problem is calculated. The responses for manufacturing firms are shown in figure 5.1.

One interesting feature of the South African data is that relatively few enterprises rated each of the constraints as a major or very severe problem. Only about 35 percent of firms rated the biggest constraint, worker skills, as a serious problem, which is far lower than the percent of firms in most countries that rated their biggest constraint as a serious problem. For example, nearly 85 percent of firms in Brazil rated the biggest problem in

Figure 5.1 Percentage of Firms Rating Investment Climate Areas as a Major or Very Severe Constraint

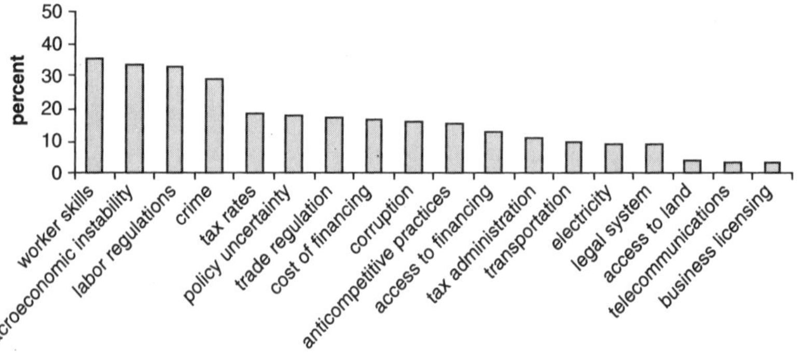

Source: Investment Climate Survey.

that country, tax rates, as a major or very severe constraint. Similarly, about 74 percent of firms in Kenya rated the biggest problem in that country, corruption, as a major or very severe constraint. This comparison suggests that enterprise managers in the South African ICS are not greatly concerned about any of the 18 areas of the investment climate.

Managers were more likely to be concerned about worker skills, macroeconomic instability, labor regulations, and crime than any other areas. Between 29 and 35 percent of enterprises rated each of these areas as a major or very severe constraint. No more than 20 percent of enterprises rated any other area as a major problem.

Ownership

Enterprises of all types were likely to rate crime as a major or very severe obstacle (table 5.1). For all groups of firms—those owned by corporations and those owned by white, Asian, or black individuals—crime ranked among the top four constraints. All groups except Asian-owned firms rated labor regulations among the top four problems. Corporate-owned firms were more likely than other firms to report macroeconomic instability as a serious problem (38 percent of enterprises), perhaps because corporate-owned firms were more likely to export (44 percent exported) than noncorporate-owned firms (26 percent) and because exporters were more concerned about macroeconomic instability. Firms owned by white individuals or families were also more likely to rate macroeconomic instability as a serious issue.

The most notable difference, however, was that black- and Asian-owned firms were far more likely to rate financial issues as major constraints than corporate- or white-owned firms. Differences related to access to finance are discussed in detail in chapter 4.

Export Status

Exporters and nonexporters generally had similar concerns. Firms in both groups were more likely to rate worker skills, macroeconomic instability, labor regulations, and crime as serious obstacles. The two most noticeable differences between exporters and nonexporters were that exporters were more concerned about macroeconomic instability and trade regulation.

Foreign Participation

The top four constraints were the same for both foreign and domestic firms. The largest difference was for access to financing, which only

Table 5.1 Percentage of Manufacturing Firms Rating Investment Climate Areas as Major or Very Severe Constraints, by Enterprise Type

	Ownership				*Export status*		*Foreign participation*	
	Corporate	*White individual*	*Asian individual*	*Black/other individual*	*Nonexporter*	*Exporter*	*Domestic*	*Foreign*
Worker skills	**44**	**30**	**29**	17	**37**	**32**	**35**	**37**
Macroeconomic instability	**38**	**33**	18	17	**28**	**44**	**33**	**37**
Labor regulations	**35**	**33**	21	**23**	**35**	**28**	**34**	**27**
Crime	**25**	**32**	**42**	**27**	**31**	**24**	**30**	**26**
Trade regulation	20	15	13	7	14	22	16	22
Policy uncertainty	19	18	11	17	16	22	17	21
Corruption	16	14	**34**	13	17	15	17	14
Anticompetitive practices	15	17	18	10	16	16	16	14
Tax rates	15	22	18	20	19	18	18	19
Cost of financing	12	19	21	**27**	17	14	17	13
Transportation	11	10	8	10	11	9	10	12
Electricity	9	9	8	3	8	11	8	14
Tax administration	7	15	8	10	12	8	11	9
Legal system	6	12	8	7	9	8	10	5
Access to financing	5	16	**32**	**27**	14	10	14	6
Access to land	5	3	5	3	4	2	4	3
Business licensing	5	3	0	7	4	2	4	3
Telecommunications	3	4	0	7	3	4	3	4

Source: Investment Climate Survey.

Note: Breakdowns only include manufacturing firms to ensure comparability across groups.

6 percent of foreign-owned enterprises but 14 percent of domestically owned enterprises rated as a serious concern.

Provincial Differences

For the most part, problems were similar across provinces (table 5.2). For three of the four provinces included in the survey—Gauteng, KwaZulu-Natal, and Western Cape—the main constraints were worker skills, labor regulations, crime, and macroeconomic instability. Enterprises in Eastern Cape ranked two of these four areas among the top constraints but were less likely to rate crime or labor regulations as a serious concern.

Enterprise managers in Eastern Cape rated trade regulation second only to macroeconomic instability as a serious problem. The concern about these two issues in the Eastern Cape might be due in part to the province's large number of exporters. Compared with nonexporters, exporters were more likely to rate both trade regulation and macroeconomic instability as a major concern.

Sector

Differences across sectors were minor. Enterprises in manufacturing, construction, and retail trade all rated worker skills, crime, and labor regulations among the four largest obstacles. The only difference was that manufacturing enterprises were far more likely to rate macroeconomic instability as a major concern than enterprises in construction or retail trade. One explanation might be that manufacturers are less domestically oriented than firms in the construction and retail trade sectors. Consistent with this reality, manufacturing enterprises with an international focus—that is, exporters and foreign-owned enterprises—were more likely to rate macroeconomic instability as a problem than domestically oriented manufacturing firms.

Major Constraints on Enterprise Operation and Growth

Two of the four constraints that enterprise managers were most likely to rate as a major or very severe obstacle are discussed in chapter 3. The other two—crime and macroeconomic instability—are discussed below.

Crime

About 30 percent of enterprises in the ICS rated crime as a major or very severe problem. Complaints about crime were common among most types of enterprise and in most regions.

Table 5.2 Percentage of Firms Rating Investment Climate Areas as Major or Very Severe Constraints, by Province and Sector

	Province				*Sector*		
	Gauteng	*KwaZulu-Natal*	*Western Cape*	*Eastern Cape*	*Manufacturing*	*Construction*	*Retail*
Worker skills	**37**	**44**	**30**	**19**	**35**	**45**	**31**
Labor regulations	**32**	**33**	**39**	17	**33**	**37**	**33**
Crime	**31**	**41**	**23**	6	**29**	**28**	**28**
Macroeconomic instability	**28**	**44**	**44**	**36**	**33**	21	18
Corruption	19	21	10	6	16	17	17
Tax rates	17	33	20	8	19	23	19
Policy uncertainty	17	27	22	0	18	19	15
Anticompetitive practices	16	25	13	8	16	15	18
Trade regulation	14	21	20	**31**	17	8	11
Cost of financing	13	24	21	**19**	16	18	13
Access to financing	12	21	12	11	13	**26**	11
Transportation	9	19	9	14	10	8	11
Electricity	9	13	5	14	9	9	2
Tax administration	8	16	18	6	11	17	**22**
Legal system	8	11	11	8	9	8	8
Telecommunications	3	6	2	6	3	4	8
Business licensing	3	5	4	3	3	4	7
Access to land	3	8	3	8	4	10	5

Source: Investment Climate Survey.

Note: Breakdowns by province include only manufacturing firms to ensure cross-region comparability.

Trends in Crime—The worst violent crimes, especially murder, have become less common in South Africa in recent years. Between 1994 and 2003, the murder rate fell by 36 percent to 0.47 murders per 1,000 people, which was similar to the rate in Washington, DC, and lower than that in Colombia, where the rate was 0.66 per 1,000 people (Leggett 2003). Property-related crime, however, has been escalating at an alarming rate. Between 1994 and 2000, common robbery rose 168 percent to 2.1 per 1,000 people, and aggravated robbery rose 31 percent to 2.7 per 1,000 people (Altbeker 2001). Since 2000, robberies and most other property crimes have continued to increase, particularly in Western Cape, where property crimes have doubled since 1994.[1]

Detailed analyses of crime in South Africa are few, but the evidence suggests that crime has a serious impact on the South African population and economy. About 44 percent of blacks and 58 percent of whites cited crime as the most serious problem facing the nation, and about one-quarter of surveyed households reported that they experienced crime in 1995 (NEDCOR 1996).

The impact of crime on business is also large. Using data from a 1999 survey of enterprises in Johannesburg, Chandra and others (2001a) report that 60 percent of businesses suffered break-ins, 40 percent suffered employee theft, and 20 percent suffered vandalism in the previous year. They find that larger firms are more likely to suffer from crime, especially break-ins, and that ethnicity is a weak predictor of victimization.

Brown (2001) presents simple correlations between local crime rates and local economic and social indicators and finds a moderate correlation between crime and the probability of prosecution—a point that he traces to the ineffectiveness of South Africa's law enforcement and criminal justice systems. According to the NEDCOR project (1996, 76, as cited in Brown 2001), "the present criminal justice system is not functioning at a level where it constitutes a credible deterrent to criminals." Brown (2001) finds moderate inverse correlations between average educational levels and crime and between average age levels and crime. Poverty, unemployment, average income, and income inequality are only weakly correlated with crime.

Crime waves are not unusual in countries undergoing transitions to democracy, particularly those with a legacy of armed resistance to authoritarian rule (Brown 2001). The increase might also partly reflect increased reporting, particularly among blacks, who had little recourse before the democratic transition. But regardless of its cause, crime in South Africa is clearly a major issue.

Crime and Security in a Comparative Perspective—Results from the ICS suggest that South Africa is representative of countries where crime and security may be considered important, though not critical, problems. In Kenya and many Latin American countries—particularly those in Central America—the security situation is likely the largest constraint to competitiveness and economic growth. South Africa's security situation is not that dire. But when compared with the security environment in other middle-income countries such as China, Lithuania, and Poland, the security environment in South Africa makes that country less attractive for foreign investment and puts South African firms at a competitive disadvantage.

About 30 percent of South African firms cite security issues as a major or severe obstacle to doing business (see figure 5.2). In this regard, South Africa compares favorably with the more volatile Latin American countries, where between 40 and 80 percent of firms rate crime as a severe obstacle. But only between 10 and 20 percent of enterprises in most middle-income countries cite security issues as a major or severe obstacle.

Objective measures of the cost of security are consistent with the perception-based data. The direct costs associated with crime are large and significant for many firms in South Africa: 0.5 percent of sales at the median (0.9 percent of value added or 2.4 percent of labor costs) and 1.2 percent of sales at the 75th percentile (see figure 5.3).[2] Consistent with the perceptions data, the cost of crime and security does not appear to be as great in South Africa as in Kenya or in the most volatile Latin

Figure 5.2 Cross-Country Comparison of Firms Rating Crime as a Serious Problem

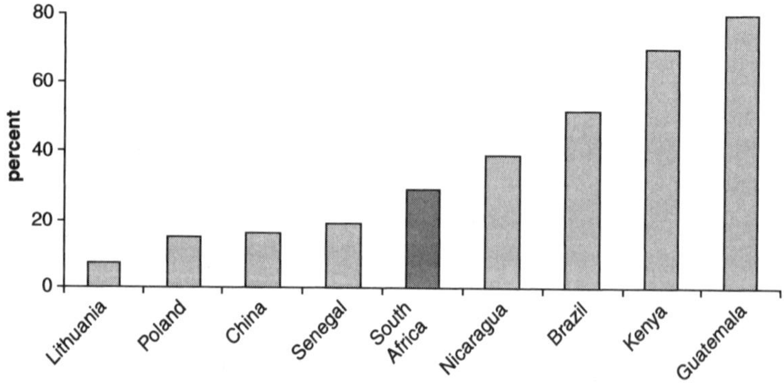

Source: Investment Climate Survey.

American countries, where firms lose 2 to 5 percent of sales at the median and 3 to 10 percent at the 75th percentile. For the median enterprise, the cost of crime in South Africa is slightly higher than that in China and Senegal and is significantly higher than that in Lithuania and Poland, where security issues cost the median firm 0 percent of sales.

Although the total cost of crime in South Africa is similar to that in other middle-income countries, the breakdown is different (figure 5.4). Few South African firms report that they make unofficial protection payments—a sharp contrast to Chinese and Polish firms, which are often forced to pay protection payments to police or organized crime. At about 40 percent, direct losses to crime and vandalism in South Africa represent

Figure 5.3 Cross-Country Comparison of Cost of Crime as a Percentage of Sales

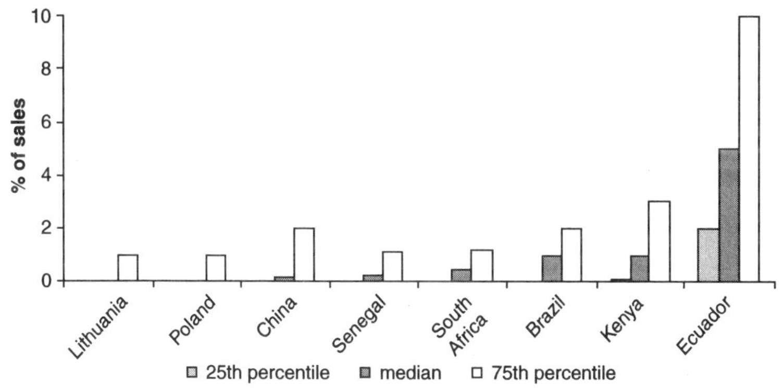

Source: Investment Climate Survey.

Figure 5.4 Cross-Country Comparison of Crime Costs, by Cost Type

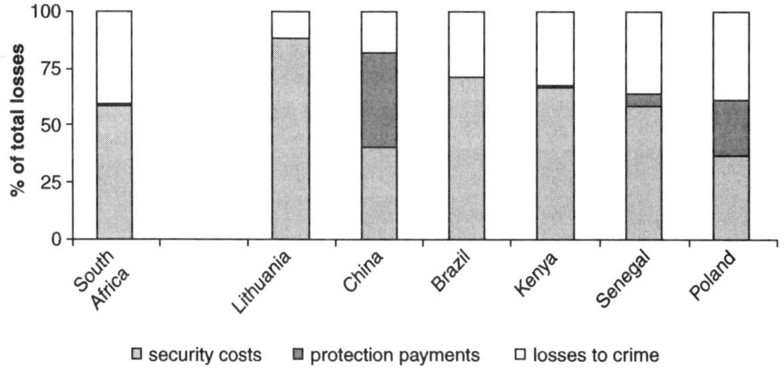

Source: Investment Climate Survey.

Figure 5.5 Cross-Country Comparison of Crime Reporting and Cases Solved

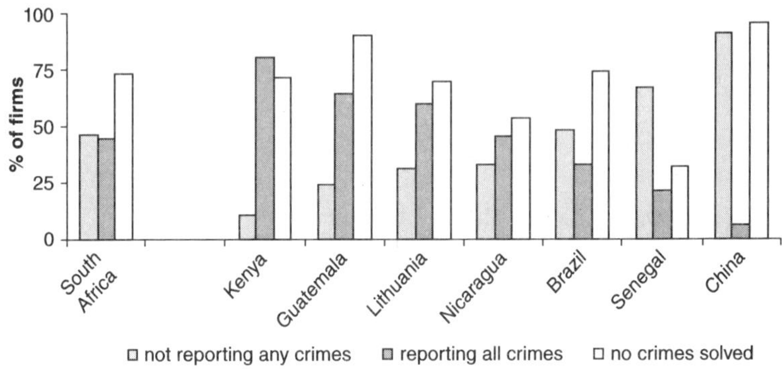

Source: Investment Climate Survey.

the largest share of total security-associated costs in any of the comparator countries, which suggests that South African firms are less effective at protecting themselves from crime than firms in other countries.

Figure 5.5 shows the degree to which firms turn to public security institutions in response to crime and the frequency with which those institutions are effective. In all countries, most firms either report all crimes or no crimes to the police, implying that reporting is a measure of trust in the effectiveness of public security. In South Africa, 44 percent of firms reported all incidents of crime and 46 percent reported none. This finding suggests that these firms have more trust in the police than firms in some of the comparator countries such as Brazil, China, and Senegal. However, 73 percent of firms reporting crimes to the police said that none of the crimes were solved. In this regard, South Africa compares unfavorably to most of the comparator countries.

Burden of Crime by Sector, Size, Location, and Ownership—The burden of crime and security is not uniform across South Africa. The data from the survey suggest that the burden of crime and security

- is relatively low for manufacturing firms and is particularly high for wholesale-retail firms,
- tends to fall disproportionately on larger firms, and
- is surprisingly moderate in Johannesburg given its reputation for crime.

The first finding is not surprising (figure 5.6). Although manufacturing firms are vulnerable to various types of crime and vandalism, converting

Figure 5.6 Total Costs of Crime and Security in South Africa, by Sector

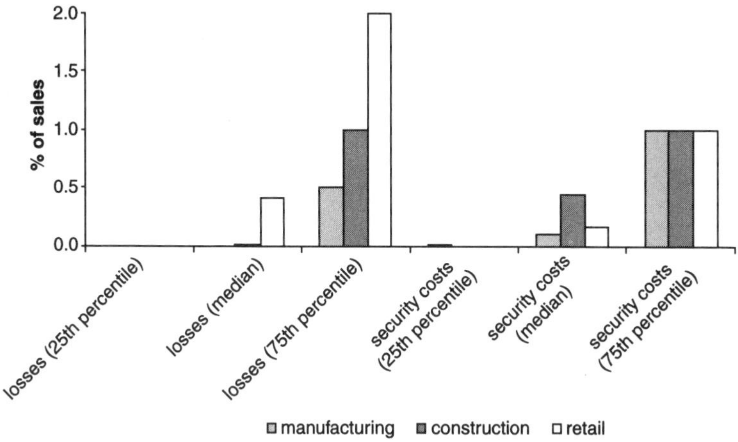

Source: Investment Climate Survey.

Table 5.3 Total Costs of Crime and Security in South Africa, by Firm Size
(percent of sales)

	Small	*Medium size*	*Large*	*Very large*
25th percentile	0.0	0.0	0.0	0.0
Median	0.2	0.2	0.5	1.0
75th percentile	1.1	1.1	1.5	2.0

Source: Authors.

their assets, raw materials, and inventories into cash is often difficult. In this respect, the inventories of wholesale and retail firms are much more enticing to thieves (including to employees, who were responsible for 21 percent of the losses in the wholesale-retail sector). Construction firms' assets (especially vehicles) are often scattered at various job sites and are therefore more vulnerable than those enclosed in factories.

The second finding is that large firms are generally more heavily burdened by crime (Chandra and others 2001a), though not uniformly so (see table 5.3). For very large firms, losses are equal to 1 percent of sales at the 50th percentile and 2 percent of sales at the 75th percentile, substantially higher at all levels than for smaller firms. Small and medium-size firms appear to face relatively similar burdens at all levels. Costs and losses for these firms appear to be more dispersed than for large firms. More small and medium-size firms escape relatively unscathed, and costs and losses tend to be lower overall. But a major crime incident can hit a small firm very hard. This pattern is similar to that in El Salvador (World Bank 2005a).

In the aggregate, crime appears to be a significant problem in most regions. Some areas have high crime (for example, Durban in KwaZulu Natal), but even firms in other regions where crime is generally viewed as a lesser problem (for example, Cape Town in Western Cape) report high losses at the median and 75th percentile. Surprisingly, firms in Gauteng province, which includes Johannesburg, generally report lower losses due to crime than firms in the other regions.

In terms of perceptions, 44 percent of firms in KwaZulu-Natal cited security and crime as a major obstacle, compared with 23 percent of firms in Western Cape, 31 percent in Gauteng, and 6 percent in Eastern Cape. A strong determinant of concern that security and crime are major obstacles is location in Durban. Although firms in Western Cape systematically face higher crime-related costs and losses than those in Gauteng, they did not rate crime as a more serious obstacle than firms in Gauteng. This finding suggests that firms' perceptions are influenced by common public perceptions of regional crime patterns.

The burden of crime varied by firm ownership, particularly along the lines of ethnicity (figure 5.7); firms owned by colored individuals incurred

Table 5.4 Total Costs of Crime and Security in South Africa, by Location
(percent of sales)

	Gauteng	*KwaZulu Natal*	*Western Cape*	*Eastern Cape*
25th percentile	0.0	0.0	0.0	0.0
Median	0.2	1.0	1.0	1.0
75th percentile	1.0	2.0	2.0	2.0

Source: Authors.

Figure 5.7 Total Costs of Crime and Security in South Africa, by Ownership

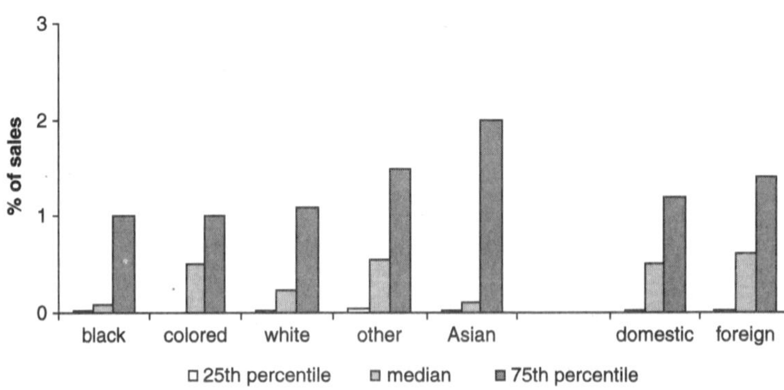

Source: Investment Climate Survey.

lower costs at the 75th percentile, and black-owned firms incurred lower costs at the median and 75th percentile than other firms. Domestic versus foreign ownership made less difference; 51 percent of domestic firms suffered criminal incidents, compared with 58 percent of foreign firms.

A more in-depth analysis suggests that ethnicity plays only a minor role when controlling for other firm characteristics, particularly in the hard data. In terms of perceptions, foreign ownership is a robust predictor that firms will cite crime as a major or severe obstacle, but white-owned firms were not significantly more likely than black-owned firms to do so.

Macroeconomic Instability

About 33 percent of South African firms rated macroeconomic instability as a serious obstacle to enterprise operations and growth—making it the second greatest constraint about which the ICS inquired. This result might be puzzling given that growth in South Africa—although not spectacular between 1993 and 2003, at least when compared with the fastest-growing economies in Asia—was not especially poor. Similarly, inflation was relatively modest. It averaged about 7 percent and was only about 4 percent in 2004.

One possible explanation for the concerns about macroeconomic instability is that, as discussed in chapter 1, exchange rates have been relatively unstable—especially against the U.S. dollar. Consistent with the idea that exchange rate instability leads firms to perceive macroeconomic instability as a problem, exporters (44 percent) were far more concerned about macroeconomic instability than nonexporters (28 percent). Because South African manufacturing firms are price takers on international markets, changes in the exchange rate can have a serious impact on enterprise revenues.

Figure 5.8 Share of Exporters Rating Macroeconomic Instability as a Serious Obstacle to Growth

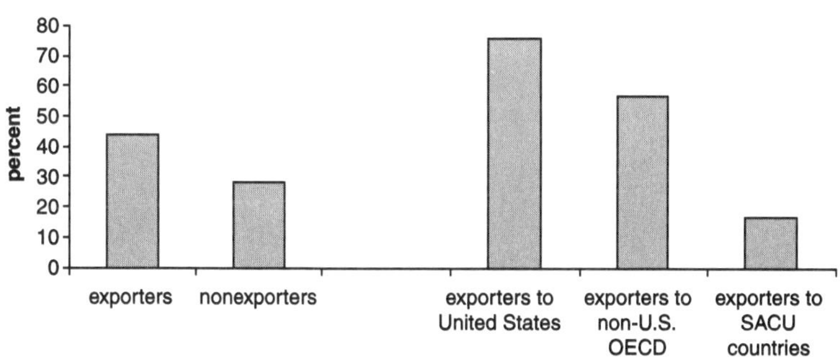

Source: Investment Climate Surveys.

Differences in perceptions among various types of exporters also suggest that concern about exchange rate instability is the main area of concern related to macroeconomic instability. About 76 percent of firms that export to the United States—the major currency against which the rand appreciated most between 2002 and 2004—viewed macroeconomic instability as a serious problem, compared with only 57 percent of firms that export to other Organisation of Economic Co-operation and Development (OECD) economies and 17 percent of firms that export to other countries in the Southern African Customs Union (SACU). Because most other countries in SACU peg their currencies against the rand, exchange rate instability would presumably be a lesser concern for enterprises that only export to other countries in SACU.

Other Constraints on Enterprise Operations and Growth

How does South Africa's performance in areas that most firms do not consider to be large constraints compare with other countries' performance?

Impact of HIV/AIDS

In addition to being a human catastrophe in terms of lost lives, HIV/AIDS undermines economic development. The HIV prevalence profile implies that the typical worker in the sectors surveyed is at the highest risk of being HIV positive. According to the Mandela study (Shisana and Simbiya 2002) and the Statistics South Africa (2004) sentinel surveillance survey, 23 percent of all South Africans above the age of 15 are HIV positive.[3] The age-specific prevalence rates are even more severe for women between the ages of 25 and 35 and for men between the ages of 30 and 40. Prevalence rates for these groups are around 30 percent. There exists a surplus pool of economically active individuals who are unemployed, but the labor supply prospects for firms appear grim in light of the average experience and embodied know-how that are likely to be lost if a significant fraction of workers become unable to work. In addition, the decline in life expectancy implies that knowledge embodied in workers through learning by doing/training is unlikely to be enduring.

Firms were asked to evaluate the impact of the HIV epidemic on four common measures of firm performance: investment, labor productivity, profit rates, and overall performance. Table 5.5 shows the percentage of firms reporting strong or prohibitive impacts on each of these measures. Nearly one-third of firms in the sample report a strong or prohibitive

Table 5.5 Impact of HIV Epidemic on Firm Performance
(percent)

Industry	*Overall*	*Investment*	*Labor productivity*	*Profit rates*
Construction	28.13	70.00	9.47	5.21
Manufacturing	32.71	44.07	6.31	3.79
Retail/wholesale	13.70	25.00	2.74	1.37
Total	30.30	45.45	6.37	3.73

Source: Authors.

impact of the epidemic on overall firm performance. The primary channel of the impact appears to be investment in light of increased uncertainty about the future productivity of workers and market size. This impact is most severe in the construction and manufacturing sectors, where 70 and 44 percent of firms, respectively, report strong or prohibitive impacts of the epidemic on investment.

Figure 5.9 shows the proportion of firms reporting strong/prohibitive impacts broken down by size class. The figure shows no discernible size-class patterns in the construction and wholesale sectors that would indicate differential ability to cope with HIV. All construction firms in the small and large size categories report strong/prohibitive impacts. However, overall and investment impacts increase with firm size in the manufacturing sector, suggesting that variation in perceived risk to firms is a function of market or firm size.

Figure 5.10 shows HIV prevalence rates reported by firms for the highly skilled, skilled, and unskilled cohorts of their respective labor forces. Prevalence rates reported by firms are considerably lower than estimates from household surveys and African National Congress sentinel surveys. In addition, the ICS results reveal a strong skill-prevalence gradient; prevalence rates among the unskilled category are more than twice as high as prevalence rates among the skilled labor category. Reported prevalence rates among the highly skilled category are very low.

Labor productivity, turnover, absenteeism, and medical expenditure have been advanced as likely channels of the adverse effects of HIV on affected economies (Bloom and Mahal 1995; Over 1992, 2001; Young 2005). Table 5.6 shows sample averages for each of these suggested channels. The modal response for each is an adverse impact that is less than 5 percent of the baseline. The impact of the epidemic is particularly severe for the construction sector, where 7.5, 11, and 22 percent firms report impacts of 10 to 20 percent on labor productivity, turnover, and absenteeism, respectively.

Figure 5.9 Impact of HIV on Firm Performance, by Size Class

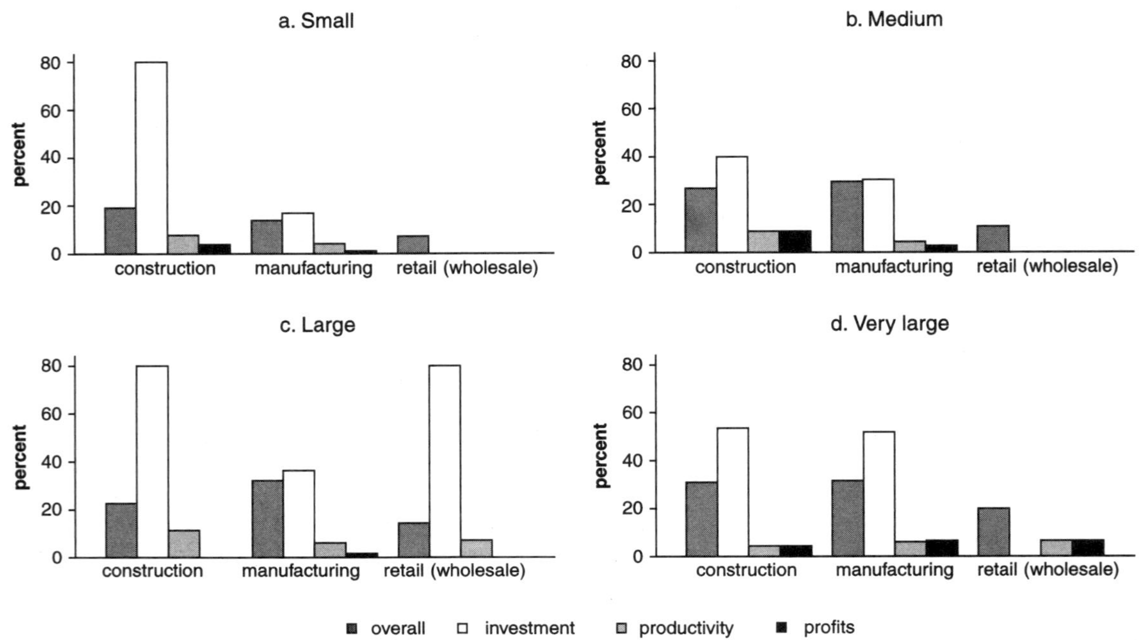

Source: Authors.

Figure 5.10 Firm-Level HIV Prevalence, by Size Class

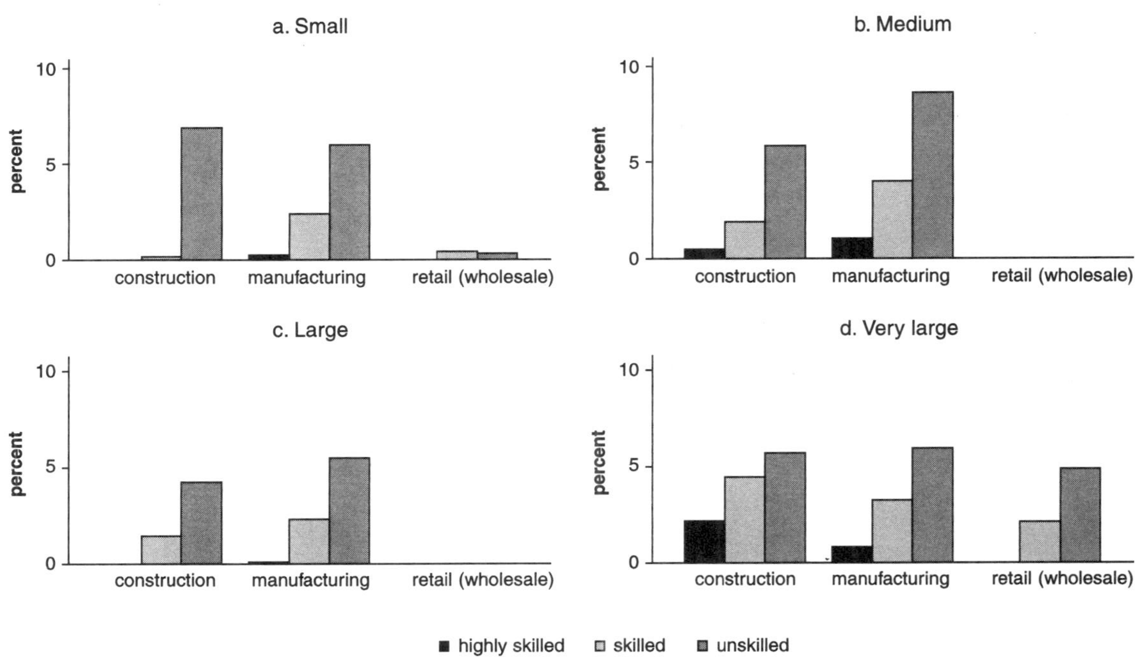

Source: Authors.

Table 5.6 Impact of HIV Epidemic

	No impact	*< 5 percent*	*5–10 percent*	*10–20 percent*	*> 20 percent*
Impact on labor productivity					
Construction	0.00	77.78	14.81	7.41	0.00
Manufacturing	9.38	78.13	9.90	1.56	1.04
Retail/wholesale	0.00	80.00	20.00	0.00	0.00
Total	***7.86***	***78.17***	***10.92***	***2.18***	***0.87***
Impact on labor turnover					
Construction	11.11	59.26	18.52	11.11	0.00
Manufacturing	9.84	78.24	6.22	3.63	2.07
Retail/wholesale	0.00	100.00	0.00	0.00	0.00
Total	***9.57***	***76.96***	***7.39***	***4.35***	***1.74***
Impact on employee absenteeism					
Construction	0.00	48.15	25.93	22.22	3.70
Manufacturing	3.63	70.47	16.58	3.63	5.70
Retail/wholesale	10.00	80.00	10.00	0.00	0.00
Total	***3.48***	***68.26***	***17.39***	***5.65***	***5.22***
Impact on medical costs					
Construction	59.26	25.93	11.11	3.70	0.00
Manufacturing	30.57	57.51	6.74	2.07	3.11
Retail/wholesale	40.00	50.00	10.00	0.00	0.00
Total	***34.35***	***53.48***	***7.39***	***2.17***	***2.61***

Source: Authors.

Only a handful of firms in the manufacturing sector report impacts of the disease on labor turnover and absenteeism that are greater than 10 percent of the baseline. Therefore, a more direct measure of worker absenteeism was examined. Workers were asked to report the number of days of work missed due to their own illness or an illness in the family in the 30 days preceding the survey. The data suggest very low levels of illness-related worker absenteeism. On average, workers missed only one day every three months, nine times lower than corresponding numbers in Central and Southern African countries with a similar HIV/AIDS burden.[4] Figure 5.11 shows the average number of days of absence due to illness for all three sectors by firm size.

Firms report lower impacts on medical costs. Just over one-third of firms report no impact on medical costs; 53 percent report an impact of less than 5 percent. These reported low impacts are likely due to the stage of the epidemic and possibly to workplace or public programs to deal with the disease.

The deviation in firm-based reports of HIV prevalence from household survey data is suggestive of the channels of the disease's impact on

Figure 5.11 Average Number of Days Absent in Last 30 Days Due to Illness, by Size Class

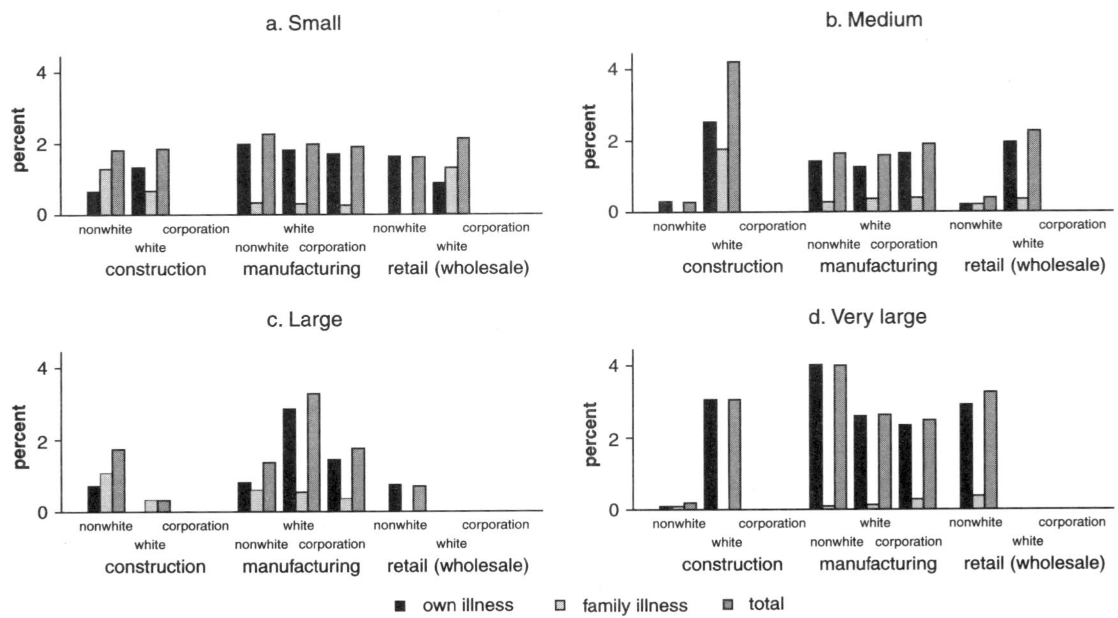

Source: Authors.

firm performance. Differences between workers in the construction, manufacturing, and retail sectors and workers in household surveys are likely to explain the substantial difference in HIV prevalence rates. This finding also underlines the fact that firms consider demand-side effects of the disease to be more important than within-firm effects.

To the extent that figures 5.9–5.12 represent firms' current perceptions of the problem, the impact of HIV on labor is likely to increase as workers with HIV progress to full-blown AIDS. A good measure of the likely trajectory of the disease and of within-firm productivity effects is suggested by worker attitudes to HIV. Figure 5.12 and table 5.7 show the percentage of workers who report HIV as an important concern, have knowledge of testing centers, and are willing to test.

Only 40 percent of workers in the construction sector report being concerned about HIV, compared with a sample average of 66 percent. Encouragingly, about 95 percent of all workers know where they can be tested for HIV. However, only half of these workers are willing to be tested. One explanation for this discrepancy may be the absence of private or public comprehensive treatment programs. Alternatively, sustained high levels of HIV stigma inhibit employees from establishing their HIV status.

Trade and Customs Regulations

Most enterprises did not view customs and trade regulations as a serious obstacle; only 16 percent rated them as a major or very severe problem. These regulations concerned exporters more than other enterprises. About 22 percent of exporters rated them as a serious obstacle—the fifth largest problem for exporters overall.

Firms were asked how long goods take to clear customs after arriving at the point of entry or exit. For the median enterprise that imported, the length was five days, compared with three days for enterprises that exported. Although goods clear customs more rapidly in South Africa than in most other countries in Sub-Saharan Africa—for example, the median firm in Kenya reports that exports take four days and imports seven days—they take longer to clear than in most of the middle-income comparator countries. For example, the median Malaysian firm reported that exports take one day and imports three days to clear customs.

Although the ICS does not allow identification of the exact point of entry and exit that each enterprise uses, firms can be identified by their location. Excluding firms that export to neighboring countries (in an attempt to ensure that they export through ports rather than through

Figure 5.12 Worker Perceptions of and Knowledge about HIV

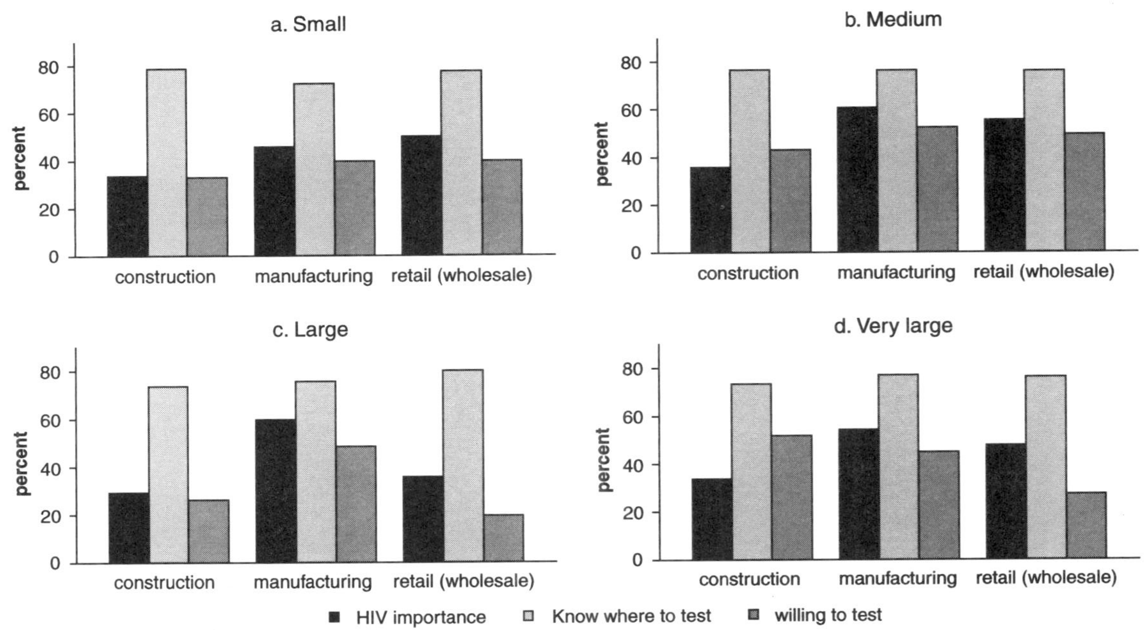

Source: Authors.

Table 5.7 Worker Perceptions about HIV Epidemic (percent)

Industry	*Believe HIV is an important concern*	*Know where to get an HIV test*	*Willing to take an HIV test*
Construction	40.57	94.27	47.58
Manufacturing	69.55	94.17	58.37
Retail/wholesale	62.00	95.97	46.07
Total	66.39	94.35	56.30

Source: Authors.

Figure 5.13 Time to Clear Imports and Exports through Customs

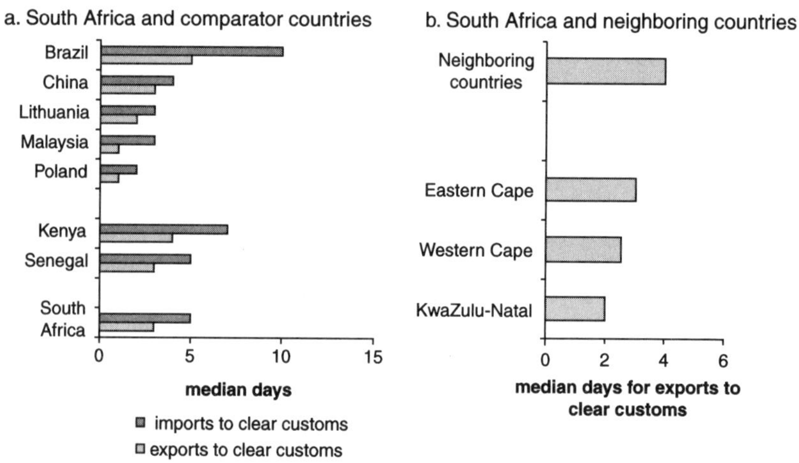

Source: Investment Climate Surveys.

land borders), figure 5.13 reports the median time to clear customs for surveyed firms from each province with port facilities. The difference among provinces appears modest. The median firm from KwaZulu-Natal reported that exports take 2 days to clear customs, compared with 2.5 days in Western Cape and 3 days in Eastern Cape. For firms that reported only neighboring countries among their export partners, customs clearance took slightly longer—four days for the median firm. Overall, these results suggest that the performance of most major port facilities is relatively good, although in all facilities it lags behind that in the best-performing middle-income countries.

Regulatory Burden

Figure 5.14 and table 5.8 show that senior managers of manufacturing firms in South Africa spend an average of 10 percent of their time dealing

Figure 5.14 Cross-Country Comparison of Regulatory Burden

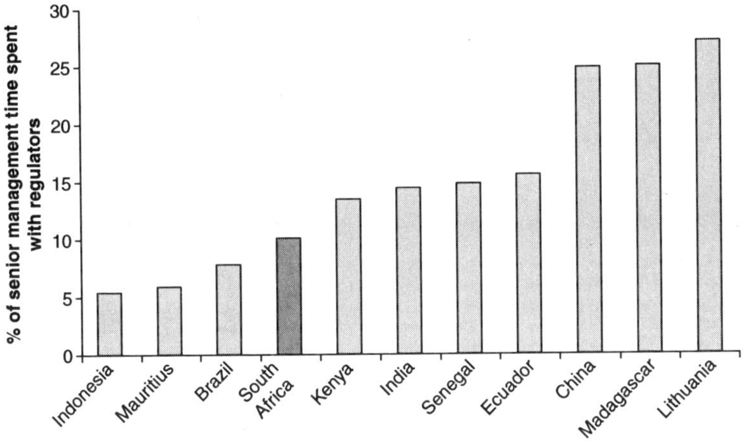

Source: Authors.

Table 5.8 Regulatory Burden for Firms

	Percent of senior management time spent on regulation	*Total number of inspection visits*
Small	9.6	3.9
Medium size	9.9	9.6
Large	10.0	15.1
Very large	8.2	14.2
Domestically owned	9.7	13.3
Foreign owned	11.8	15.1
Nonexporter	9.9	9.6
Exporter	10.4	18.8
Total	***10.1***	***13.7***

Source: Authors.

with regulatory officials and regulations. The average time spent with regulations is uniform across different categories of firms. The regulatory burden that firms in South Africa face is less than that faced by firms in many middle-income countries.

One measure of regulatory burden is the average number of regulators' inspections. The average number of inspections in South African firms is equivalent to about one per month. Larger and exporting firms are subject to a higher number of inspections. Exporting firms experience twice as many inspections as nonexporting firms.

Courts and Property Rights

Firms were asked how confident they were that the judicial system would enforce their contractual property rights in business disputes. Figure 5.15 shows the average response; 0 indicates strong disagreement and 6 indicates strong agreement. As the figure shows, manufacturing firms are generally confident in the judicial system, and nonexporting firms are more confident than exporting firms. Of potential concern is the average response of the micro firms in the survey. On average, these firms are unsure if they could use the judicial system to resolve disputes, probably because the cost of doing so is potentially prohibitive.

The median time required to resolve business disputes is four weeks (table 5.9). Variation in case duration is significant, as evidenced by the average, which is about six times as long as the median court time. On the other hand, court cases are resolved more quickly in South Africa

Figure 5.15 Firms' Confidence That Courts Will Enforce Rights

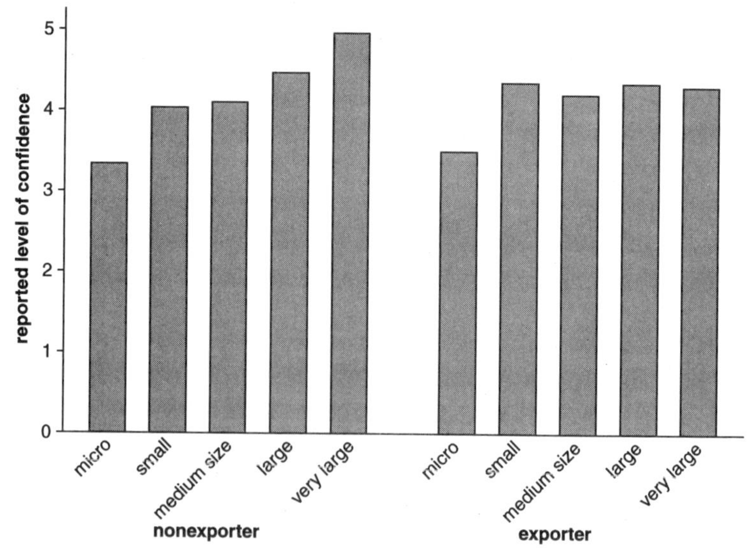

Source: Authors.
Note: 0 = no confidence; 5 = high confidence.

Table 5.9 Time Courts Take to Resolve Business Disputes

Firm size	*Average, weeks*	*Median, weeks*
Small	19.40	7.50
Medium size	12.27	1.00
Large	23.03	7.00
Very large	36.59	1.50

Source: Authors.

than in many competing middle-income economies. For example, courts in Brazil take 2.5 times as long to resolve cases than courts in South Africa. Courts in China take about the same time as those in South Africa (see figure 5.16).

Power

The average share of electricity in manufacturing costs is just under 3 percent, which is considerably lower than corresponding cost shares in many competing economies. Figure 5.17 shows that median shares of electricity in Indonesia and Malaysia are twice as large as those in South Africa.

Figure 5.16 Cross-Country Comparison of Weeks to Resolve Overdue Payment Cases in Courts

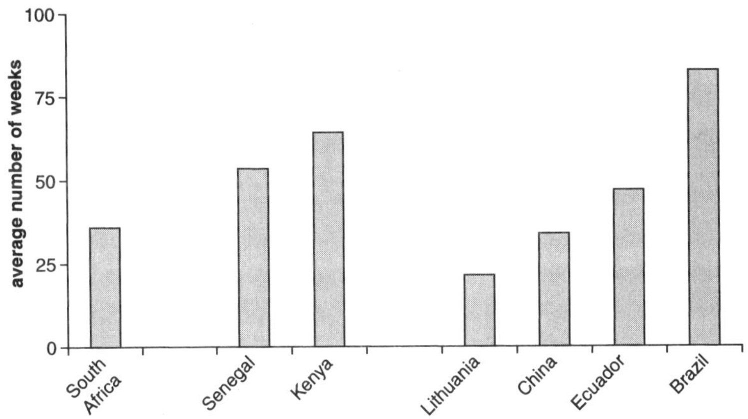

Source: Authors.

Figure 5.17 Cross-Country Comparison of Median Energy Costs as Percent of Sales

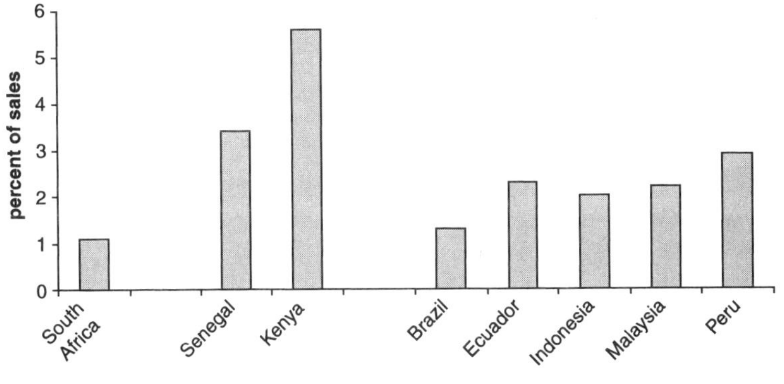

Source: Authors.

Electricity is not only relatively cheap but also reliable in South Africa. Figure 5.18 shows the percentage of output lost due to power outages. Nonexporting firms experience more unreliable power supply than exporting firms, probably due to differences in location.

The output loss due to electricity outages for manufacturing firms in South Africa—less than 1 percent—is lower than that for manufacturing firms in all the comparator countries. The average output lost in South Africa is about half of the output fraction lost due to poor power supply in China and Indonesia.

As a result of reliable electricity supply, South African firms are less likely to own a generator than firms in comparator countries. An average of 9.5 percent of South African firms own a generator, compared with 18 percent of Chinese firms, 22 percent of Lithuanian firms, and 39 percent of Indonesian firms.

Taxation

Most surveyed enterprises in South Africa did not view taxation as a major problem. Only 19 percent of enterprises considered tax rates a serious problem, and only 11 percent considered tax administration a serious problem. Although tax rates ranked as the fifth greatest obstacle overall, the gap between the fourth and fifth rated obstacles was large. Moreover, tax rates were typically viewed as a serious obstacle in the 52 countries where Investment Climate Surveys had been completed by mid-2005;

Figure 5.18 Cross-Country Comparison of Average Losses Due to Power Outages as Percent of Sales

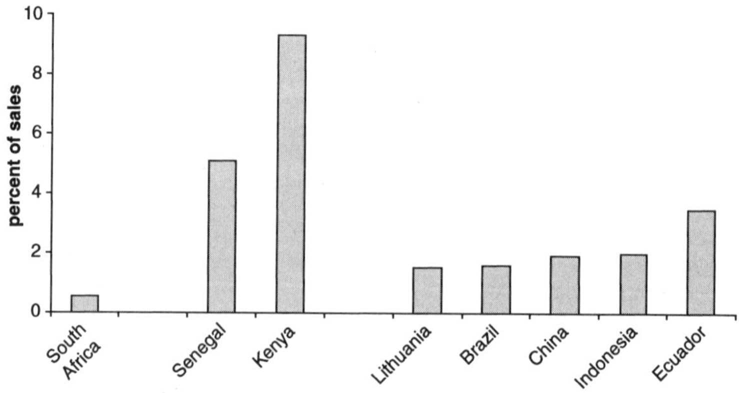

Source: Authors.

Table 5.10 Company Income Tax, 1994/5–2003/4

Year	*CIT rand (million)*	*Year-to-year change*	*Percent of tax revenue*	*Percent of GDP*
1994/95	13 777	18.9	12.1	2.8
1995/96	15 831	14.9	12.4	2.8
1996/97	19 060	20.4	12.9	3.0
1997/98	21 609	13.4	13.1	3.1
1998/99	22 822	5.6	12.3	3.0
1999/2000	21 279	(6.8)	10.6	2.6
2000/01	29 956	40.8	13.6	3.3
2001/02	42 979	43.5	17.0	4.3
2002/03	56 326	31.1	20.0	4.9
2003/04	61 712	9.6	20.4	5.0
2004/05	71 629	16.1	20.2	5.0
2005/06	87 326	21.9	21.0	5.5

Source: South African Revenue Services 2006, 15.
Note: CIT comprises all provisional and assessed taxes paid by companies (net of refunds).

compared with South African enterprises, enterprises in only 3 of these countries were less likely to say tax rates were a serious obstacle.[5]

Since 1994/95 the amount of income tax paid by South African companies has expanded at a rapid rate (table 5.10). The only exception was 1998/99, when economic growth and company profits plummeted following the Asian financial crisis. Company Income Tax (CIT) consistently increased as a share of total tax revenue from 1994 to 2006 and was close to 22 percent of total revenue by 2005/06. As a share of GDP, CIT increased from around 3 percent in the mid-1990s to 5.5 percent in 2005/06.

The corporate tax rate was 35 percent until 1998, when it decreased to 30 percent. In the 2005 budget, the corporate tax rate fell to 29 percent. Despite this significant reduction, tax revenues increased substantially. From a base of 100 in 1995, revenue derived from taxes on companies doubled to 200.8 in 2000–01 and more than doubled to 410.9 in 2003 (Chamsa 2004, 10). The robust growth in CIT is a consequence not only of increased company profitability but also of improved enforcement and compliance and a considerable increase in the company register.[6] In addition to CIT, South African companies pay Secondary Tax on Companies (STC), a tax on the profits that they distribute. The STC share of tax revenue increased from about 1 percent in the mid-1990s to a little over 2 percent in recent years. As a share of GDP, STC increased from around 0.2 percent in the mid-1990s to 0.5 percent in 2003–04 (South African Revenue Services 2004, 16).

Notes

1. Leggett (2003) notes that government officials cite fraudulent theft claims as potentially responsible for rising crime statistics but finds that the falling rate of reported fraud cases undermines this explanation.
2. At the median, net value added and labor costs are 54 and 21 percent of sales, respectively. Although many figures on the cost of crime are given here in terms of sales, considering the impacts relative to value added and labor costs may be intuitive.
3. National estimates for HIV prevalence from the Mandela study are likely to be biased due to nonresponse rates of between 30 and 40 percent of sampled individuals.
4. Central and East Africa have a much higher malaria burden than South Africa, which could account for the difference in sources of worker absenteeism.
5. Data are available from the World Bank rapid response Web site: http://rru.worldbank.org/.
6. The number of companies on the register increased by almost 20 percent from 2001 to 2004 (South African Revenue Services 2004, 24).

References

Altbeker, Anthony. 2001. "Losing Our Nerve? Business Confidence and Crime in South Africa." *Nedbank ISS Crime Index* 5 (4). Available at http://www.iss.co.za/Publications/Crimeindex.html.

Aw, Bee Yan, Sukkyun Chung, and Mark J. Roberts. 2000. "Productivity and Turnover in the Export Market: Micro-Level Evidence from the Republic of Korea and Taiwan (China)." *World Bank Economic Review* 14 (1): 65–90.

Behar, Alberto, and Lawrence Edwards. 2004. "Estimating Elasticities of Demand and Supply for South African Manufactured Exports Using a Vector Error Correction Model." Development and Comp Systems, EconWPA.

———. 2006. "Trade Liberalization and Labour Demand within South African Manufacturing Firms." *Journal for Studies in Economics and Econometrics* 30 (2): 1–20.

Bell, Trevor, and Niki Cattaneo. 1997. "Foreign Trade and Employment in the South African Manufacturing Industry." Occasional Report 4, Employment and Training Department, *International Labour Office*, Geneva.

Bernard, Andrew B., and J. Bradford Jensen. 1999. "Exceptional Exporter Performance: Cause, Effect, or Both?" *Journal of International Economics* 47 (1): 1–25.

Bhorat, Haroon. 1999. "Decomposing Sectoral Employment Trends in South Africa." Paper presented at the Trade and Industrial Policy Secretariat Annual Forum, Muldersdrift, September.

Bhorat, Haroon, and Paul Lundall. 2004. "Employment and Labor Market Effects of Globalization: Selected Issues for Policy Management." International Labour Organization, Geneva.

Birdi, Alvin, Paul Dunne, and Duncan Watson. 2001. "Labor Demand and Trade in South Africa: A Dynamic Panel Analysis." Paper presented at the Annual Conference on Econometric Modeling for Africa, Pretoria, July.

Blattman, Christopher, Jason Hwang, and Jeffrey G. Williamson. 2004. "The Impact of the Terms of Trade on Economic Development in the Periphery, 1870–1939: Volatility and Secular Change." Working Paper 10600, National Bureau of Economic Research, Cambridge, MA.

Bloom, David, and Ajay Mahal. 1997. "Does the AIDS Epidemic Threaten Economic Growth?" *Journal of Econometrics* 77 (1): 105–24.

Boccara, Bruno, and Peter Moll. 1997. "Labor Market Flexibility and Industrial Councils in South Africa." Mimeo, Africa Region, World Bank, Washington, DC.

Brown, Kay. 2001. "The Determinants of Crime in South Africa." *South African Journal of Economics* 69 (2): 269–98.

Brown, Mercy, David Kaplan, and Jean-Baptiste Meyer. 2002. "The Brain Drain: An Outline of Skilled Emigration from South Africa." In *Destinations Unknown: Perspectives on the Brain Drain in Southern Africa*, ed. David A McDonald and Jonathan Crush, 99–112. Pretoria: Africa Institute of South Africa.

Business Monitor International. 2005. "South Africa Left Behind." January.

Butcher, Kristin, and Cecilia Rouse. 2001. "Wage Effects of Unions and Industrial Councils in South Africa." *Industrial and Labor Relations Review* 54 (2): 349–74.

Case, Anne, and Angus Deaton. 1999. "School Inputs and Educational Outcomes in South Africa." *Quarterly Journal of Economics* 114 (3): 1047–84.

Chambers of Commerce and Industry South Africa (Chamsa). 2004. *Economic and Intelligence Quarterly* 1 (4).

Chandra, Vandana, Lalita Moorty, Bala Rajaratnam, and Kendall Schaefer. 2001a. "Constraints to Growth and Employment in South Africa: Statistics from the Large Manufacturing Firm Survey." Discussion Paper 14. World Bank, Washington, DC.

Chandra, Vandana, Lalita Moorty, Jean-Pascal Nganou, Bala Rajaratnam, and Kendall Schaefer. 2001b. "Constraints to Growth and Employment in South Africa—Report No. 2: Evidence from the Small, Medium and Micro Enterprise Survey." Informal Discussion Paper 15. World Bank, Washington, DC.

Chandra, Vandana, Jean-Pascal Nganou, and Claire Marie-Noel. 2002. "South Africa: Constraints to Growth in Johannesburg's Black Informal Sector: Evidence from the 1999 Informal Sector Survey." Washington, DC: World Bank.

Clerides, Sofronis K., Saul Lach, and James R. Tybout. 1998. "Is Learning by Exporting Important? Micro-dynamic Evidence from Colombia, Mexico, and Morocco." *Quarterly Journal of Economics* 113 (3): 903–47.

Cotton, Linda, James Habyarimana, Chad Leechor, Jean Michel Marchat, John Paton, Vijaya Ramachandran, Manju Kedia Shah, Michael Wong, William Kalema, and Charles Ntale. 2004. "Competing in the Global Economy: An Investment Climate Assessment for Uganda." Regional Program for Enterprise Development, World Bank, Washington, DC.

Demombynes, Gabriel, and Berk Ozler. 2005. "Crime and Local Inequality in South Africa." *Journal of Development Economics* 76 (2): 265–92.

Dollar, David, Shualin Wang, Lixin Colin Xu, and Anqing Shi. 2005. "Improving City Competitiveness through the Investment Climate: Ranking 23 Chinese Cities." China Finance and Economics Press, Beijing.

Edwards, Lawrence. 2005. "South Africa's Export Performance: Determinants of Export Supply." Informal Discussion Paper Series on South Africa 2005/03. World Bank, Pretoria.

Edwards, Lawrence, and Stephen S. Golub. 2003. "South African Productivity and Capital Accumulation in Manufacturing: An International Comparative Analysis." *South African Journal of Economics* 71 (4): 659–79.

Edwards, Lawrence, and Stephen Golub. 2004. "South Africa's International Cost Competitiveness and Productivity in Manufacturing." *World Development* 32 (8): 1323–39.

Edwards, Lawrence, and Tijl van de Winkel. 2005. "The Market Disciplining Effects of Trade Liberalization and Regional Import Penetration on Manufacturing in South Africa." Working Paper 1-2005, Trade and Industrial Policy Strategies, Pretoria.

Fedderke, Johannes. 2005. "South Africa: Sources and Constraints of Long-Term Growth, 1970–2000." Informal Discussion Paper Series on South Africa 2005/01, World Bank, Pretoria.

Fedderke, Johannes, Raphael de Kadt, and John M. Luiz. 2000. "Uneducating South Africa: The Failure to Address the 1910–1993 Legacy." *International Review of Education* 46 (3/4): 257–81.

Fedderke, Johannes, Chandana Kularatne, and Martine Mariotti. 2003. "Mark-up Pricing in South African Industry." Economic Research Southern Africa Working Paper No. 1, University of Cape Town, Cape Town.

Fedderke, J. W., Y. Shin, and P. Vaze. 2003. "Trade and Labor Usage: An Examination of the South African Manufacturing Industry." Working Paper 15, Econometric Research Southern Africa, University of Witwatersrand, Johannesburg.

Fedderke, Johannes, and Gabor Szalontai. 2005. "Industry Concentration in South African Manufacturing: Trends and Consequences, 1972–1996." World Bank Informal Discussion Paper Series on South Africa 2005/02. World Bank, Pretoria.

Financial Mail. 2005. "Growth Picks Up in 2004 but Average Year Awaits." February 18.

Gelb, Stephen. 2001. "Fixed Investment in South Africa." Office of the President, Government of the Republic of South Africa, Pretoria.

———. 2004a. "An Overview of the South African Economy." In *State of the Nation: South Africa 2004–2005*, ed. John Daniel, Adam Habib, and Roger Southall, 367–400. Pretoria: HSRC Press.

———. 2004b. "Economic Growth and Development: The Framework for Empowerment." In *Taking Power in the Economy: Gains and Directions*. The Institute for Justice and Reconciliation: Economic Transformation Audit.

Government of South Africa. 1996. "Growth, Employment and Redistribution: A Macroeconomic Strategy." http://www.polity.org.za/html/govdocs/policy/growth.html.

Hinkle, Lawrence, and Peter J. Montiel. 1999. *Exchange Rate Misalignment: Concepts and Measurement for Developing Countries*. Oxford, UK: Oxford University Press.

Hoekman, Bernard, Hiau Looi Kee, and Marcelo Olarreaga. 2001. "Markups, Entry Regulations, and Trade: Does Country Size Matter?" Policy Research Working Paper 2662, World Bank, Washington, DC.

Hudson, Judi. 2003. "RIAS and Private Sector Development: Some Thoughts from the South African Context." Small Business Project, Johannesburg, South Africa.

IMF (International Monetary Fund). 2004. South Africa: 2004 Article IV Consultation—Staff Report; Staff Statement; and Public Information Notice on the Executive Board Discussion. International Monetary Fund, Washington, DC.

———. 2004. *International Finance Statistics*. Washington, DC: IMF.

Kaplan, David. 2004. "Manufacturing in South Africa over the Last Decade: A Review of Industrial Performance and Policy." *Development Southern Africa* 21(4): 623–44.

Kaplinsky, Raphael. 1995. "Capital Intensity in South African Manufacturing and Unemployment." *World Development* 23 (2): 179–92.

Kee, Hiau Looi, and Bernard Hoekman. 2003. "Imports, Entry, and Competition Law as Market Disciplines." Policy Research Working Paper 3031, World Bank, Washington, DC.

Keller, Wolfgang. 2003. "International Technology Diffusion." Department of Economics, University of Texas, Austin.

Kumbhakar, Subal C., and C. A. Knox Lovell. 2000. *Stochastic Frontier Analysis*. Cambridge: Cambridge University Press.

Leggett, Ted. 2003. "The Facts behind the Figures: Crime Statistics 2002/03." *South African Crime Quarterly* 6 (4): 1–5.

Levy, Brian. 1992. "How Can South African Manufacturing Efficiently Create Employment? An Analysis of the Impact of Trade and Industrial Policy." Informal Discussion Paper on Aspects of the Economy of South Africa 1, World Bank, Washington, DC.

Lewis, H. Gregg. 1963. *Unionism and Relative Wages in the United States*. Chicago: University of Chicago Press.

Liu, Jin-Tan, Meng-Wen Tsou, and James K. Hammitt. 1999. "Export Activity and Productivity: Evidence from the Taiwan Electronics Industry." *Weltwirtschaftliches Archiv* 135 (4): 675–91.

Mazumdar, D., and D. van Seventer. 2004. "A Decomposition of Growth of the Real Wage Rate for South Africa, 1970–2000." *South African Journal of Economics* 70 (6): 1076–1102.

Mbaye, Ahmadou Aly, and Stephen Golub. 2003. "Unit Labour Costs, International Competitiveness, and Exports: The Case of Senegal." *Journal of African Economics* 11 (2): 219–48.

Mincer, Jacob. 1974. *Schooling, Experience, and Earnings*. New York: Columbia University Press for the National Bureau for Economic Research.

Moll. 1991. "Better Schools or More Schools: The Equity-Growth Trade-off in South African Education." *Journal for Studies in Economics and Econometrics* 15 (1): 1–10.

Mwabu, G. M., and T. P. Shultz. 1996. "Wage Premia for Education and Location, by Gender and Race in South Africa." *Economic Development and Cultural Change* 48 (2): 307–34.

National Treasury (South Africa). 2004. *Tax Policy in South Africa*. Presentation to the National Economic Development and Labour Council. Public Finance and Monetary Policy Chamber, Pretoria.

National Treasury (South Africa). 2005a. *Budget Review*. Pretoria.

National Treasury (South Africa). 2005b. "South Africa's Growth and Development: Overview." National Treasury Growth Diagnostics Workshop, Pretoria, March 31.

Nattrass, Nicoli. 1998. "Globalisation, Employment and Labour Market Institutions in South Africa." Working Paper 14, South African Network for Economic Research, Cape Town.

———. 2003. "The State of the Economy: A Crisis of Unemployment." In *State of the Nation: South Africa 2003–2004*, ed. John Daniel, Adam Habib, and Roger Southall, 141–57. Pretoria: HSRC Press.

———. 2004. "Unemployment and Aids: The Social-Democratic Challenge for South Africa." *Development South Africa* 21 (1): 87–108.

NEDCOR. 1996. "The NEDCOR Project on Crime, Violence and Investment." Johannesburg, South Africa.

Over, Mead. 1992. "The Macroeconomic Impact of AIDS in Sub-Saharan Africa." Technical Working Paper No. 3, Population and Human Resources Department, World Bank.

———. 2001. "The Macroeconomic Impact of AIDS in Sub-Saharan Africa." World Bank, Washington, DC.

Pencavel, John. 1995. *The Role of Labor Unions in Fostering Economic Development*. Washington, DC: World Bank.

PURE (Public Funding and Private Returns to Education). 2001. Center for European Economic Research, European Commission, Frankfurt,.

Rospabe, Sandrine. 1999. "How did Labor Market Racial Discrimination Evolve after the End of Apartheid? An Analysis of the Evolution of Hiring, Occupational and Wage Discrimination in South Africa between 1993 and 1999." Draft, University of Cape Town.

Selod, Harris, and Yves Zenou. 2003. "Private versus Public Schools in Post-Apartheid South African Cities: Theory and Policy Implications." *Journal of Development Economics* 71 (2): 351–94.

Shisana, Olive, and Leickness Chisamu Simbayi. 2002. "Nelson Mandela/HSRC Study of HIV/AIDS, South African National HIV Prevalence, Behavioural Risks and Mass Media: Household Survey 2002." Human Sciences Research Council, Cape Town.

South African Revenue Service. 2004. *Annual Report*. Pretoria: South African Revenue Service.

———. 2006. *Annual Report*. Pretoria: South African Revenue Service.

South African Reserve Bank. 2002 (June). "Quarterly Bulletin." South African Reserve Bank, Pretoria.

———. 2004a (September). "Quarterly Bulletin." South African Reserve Bank, Pretoria.

———. 2004b (December). "Quarterly Bulletin." South African Reserve Bank, Pretoria.

Statistics South Africa. 2003–05 (various editions). *South African Statistics*. Pretoria: Statistics South Africa.

———. 2004 (December). "Bulletin of Statistics." Statistics South Africa, Pretoria.

Stern, Nicholas. 2002a. "Development as a Process of Change." Office of the Chief Economist, Development Economics, World Bank, Washington, DC.

———. 2002b. *A Strategy for Development*. Washington, DC: World Bank.

Tybout, James R. 2003. "Plant- and Firm-Level Evidence on 'New' Trade Theories." In *Handbook of International Trade*, ed. E. Kwan Choi and James Harrigan, 389–415. Malden, MA: Blackwell.

UNDP (United Nations Development Programme). 2003. *South African Human Development Report 2003: The Challenge of Sustainable Development: Unlocking People's Creativity*. Oxford, UK: Oxford University Press.

Westphal, Larry E. 2002. "Technology Strategies for Economic Development in a Fast Changing Global Economy." *Economics of Innovation and New Technology* 11 (4–5): 275–320.

World Bank. 2004a. "Investment Climate Assessment: Enterprise Performance and Growth in Tanzania." Regional Program on Enterprise Development, Africa Private Sector Group, World Bank, Washington, DC.

———. 2004b. *World Development Report 2005: A Better Investment Climate for Everyone*. Washington, DC: World Bank.

———. 2004c. "Enhancing the Competitiveness of Kenya's Manufacturing Sector: The Role of the Investment Climate." Regional Program on Enterprise Development, Africa Private Sector Group, World Bank, Washington, DC.

———. 2004d. *Doing Business in 2005*. World Bank: Washington, DC.

———. 2005a. "El Salvador: Investment Climate Assessment." Development Economics Research Group (DECRG) and Finance, Private Sector and Infrastructure, Latin America and the Caribbean Region (LCSFR), World Bank, Washington, DC.

———. 2005b. *World Development Indicators*. Washington, DC: World Bank.

Young, A. 2005. "The Gift of the Dying: The Tragedy of AIDS and the Welfare of Future African Generations." *Quarterly Journal of Economics* 120: 243–66.

Index

Notes are indicated by n.

ECO-AUDIT

Environmental Benefits Statement

The World Bank is committed to preserving endangered forests and natural resources. The Office of the Publisher has chosen to print ***An Assessment of the Investment Climate in South Africa*** on recycled paper with 30 percent postconsumer fiber in accordance with the recommended standards for paper usage set by the Green Press Initiative, a nonprofit program supporting publishers in using fiber that is not sourced from endangered forests. For more information, visit www.greenpressinitiative.org.

Saved:

- 3 trees
- 2 million BTUs of total energy
- 271 lbs. CO_2 equivalent of greenhouse gases
- 1,126 gallons of wastewater
- 145 pounds of solid waste

green press INITIATIVE